Image and Video Matting: A Survey

Image and Video Matting: A Survey

Jue Wang

Adobe Systems Incorporated
801 North 34th Street
Seattle, WA 98103
USA

juewang@adobe.com

Michael F. Cohen

Microsoft Research
One Microsoft Way
Redmond, WA 98052
USA

michael.cohen@microsoft.com

the essence of knowledge

Boston – Delft

Foundations and Trends® in Computer Graphics and Vision

Published, sold and distributed by:
now Publishers Inc.
PO Box 1024
Hanover, MA 02339
USA
Tel. +1-781-985-4510
www.nowpublishers.com
sales@nowpublishers.com

Outside North America:
now Publishers Inc.
PO Box 179
2600 AD Delft
The Netherlands
Tel. +31-6-51115274

The preferred citation for this publication is J. Wang and M. F. Cohen, Image and Video Matting: A Survey, Foundations and Trends® in Computer Graphics and Vision, vol 3, no 2, pp 97–180, 2007

ISBN: 978-1-60198-134-9

Editorial Scope

Foundations and Trends® in Computer Graphics and Vision will publish survey and tutorial articles in the following topics:

- Rendering: Lighting models; Forward rendering; Inverse rendering; Image-based rendering; Non-photorealistic rendering; Graphics hardware; Visibility computation
- Shape: Surface reconstruction; Range imaging; Geometric modelling; Parameterization;
- Mesh simplification
- Animation: Motion capture and processing; Physics-based modelling; Character animation
- Sensors and sensing
- Image restoration and enhancement
- Segmentation and grouping
- Feature detection and selection
- Color processing
- Texture analysis and synthesis
- Illumination and reflectance modeling
- Shape Representation
- Tracking
- Calibration
- Structure from motion
- Motion estimation and registration
- Stereo matching and reconstruction
- 3D reconstruction and image-based modeling
- Learning and statistical methods
- Appearance-based matching
- Object and scene recognition
- Face detection and recognition
- Activity and gesture recognition
- Image and Video Retrieval
- Video analysis and event recognition
- Medical Image Analysis
- Robot Localization and Navigation

Information for Librarians

Foundations and Trends® in Computer Graphics and Vision, 2007, Volume 3, 4 issues. ISSN paper version 1572-2740. ISSN online version 1572-2759. Also available as a combined paper and online subscription.

Foundations and Trends® in
Computer Graphics and Vision
Vol. 3, No. 2 (2007) 97–180

DOI: 10.1561/0600000019

Image and Video Matting: A Survey

Jue Wang[1] and Michael F. Cohen[2]

[1] *Adobe Systems Incorporated, 801 North 34th Street, Seattle, WA 98103, USA, juewang@adobe.com*
[2] *Microsoft Research, One Microsoft Way, Redmond, WA 98052, USA, michael.cohen@microsoft.com*

Abstract

Matting refers to the problem of accurate foreground estimation in images and video. It is one of the key techniques in many image editing and film production applications, thus has been extensively studied in the literature. With the recent advances of digital cameras, using matting techniques to create novel composites or facilitate other editing tasks has gained increasing interest from both professionals as well as consumers. Consequently, various matting techniques and systems have been proposed to try to efficiently extract high quality mattes from both still images and video sequences.

This survey provides a comprehensive review of existing image and video matting algorithms and systems, with an emphasis on the advanced techniques that have been recently proposed. The first part of the survey is focused on image matting. The fundamental techniques shared by many image matting algorithms, such as color sampling methods and matting affinities, are first analyzed. Image matting techniques are then classified into three categories based on their underlying methodologies, and an objective evaluation is conducted to reveal the advantages and disadvantages of each category. A unique Accuracy vs. Cost analysis is presented as a practical guidance for readers to properly choose matting tools that best fit their specific requirements and constraints.

The second part of the survey is focused on video matting. The difficulties and challenges of video matting are first analyzed, and various ways of combining matting algorithms with other video processing techniques for building efficient video matting systems are reviewed. Key contributions, advantages as well as limitations of important systems are summarized.

Finally, special matting systems that rely on capturing additional foreground/background information to automate the matting process are discussed. A few interesting directions for future matting research are presented in the conclusion.

Contents

1

Introduction

1.1 The Matting Problem

Extracting foreground objects from still images or video sequences plays an important role in many image and video editing applications, thus it has been extensively studied for more than 20 years. Accurately separating a foreground object from the background involves determining both full and partial pixel coverage, also known as *pulling a matte*, or *foreground matting*. This problem was mathematically established by Porter and Duff in 1984 [29]. They introduced the alpha channel as the means to control the linear interpolation of foreground and background colors for anti-aliasing purposes when rendering a foreground over an arbitrary background. Mathematically, the observed image I_z ($z = (x, y)$) is modeled as a convex combination of a foreground image F_z and a background image B_z by using the alpha matte α_z:

$$I_z = \alpha_z F_z + (1 - \alpha_z) B_z, \tag{1.1}$$

where α_z can be any value in [0,1]. If $\alpha_z = 1$ or 0, we call pixel z *definite foreground* or *definite background*, respectively. Otherwise we call pixel z *mixed*. In most natural images, although the majority of pixels are either definite foreground or definite background, accurately estimating alpha values for mixed pixels is essential for fully separating the foreground from the background.

Given only a single input image, all three values α, F, and B are unknown and need to be determined at every pixel location. The known information we have for a pixel are the three dimensional color vector I_z (assuming it is represented in some 3D color space), and the unknown variables are the three dimensional color vectors F_z and B_z, and the scalar alpha value α_z. Matting is thus inherently an under-constrained problem, since 7 unknown variables need to be estimated from 3 known values. Most matting approaches rely on user guidance and prior assumptions on image statistics to constrain the problem to obtain good estimates of the unknown variables. Once estimated correctly, the foreground can be seamlessly composed onto a new background, by simply replacing the original background B with a new background image B' in Equation (1.1).

1.2 Binary Segmentation vs. Matting

If we constrain the alpha values to be only 0 or 1 in Equation (1.1), the matting problem then degrades to another classic problem: binary image/video segmentation, where each pixel fully belongs to either foreground or background. This problem has been extensively studied since early 1960s, resulting in a large volume of related literature. Although matting is modeled as a more general problem than binary segmentation, which is theoretically harder to solve, most existing matting algorithms avoid the segmentation problem by having a *trimap* as another input in addition to the original image. The trimap may be manually specified by the user, or produced by other binary segmentation approaches. The trimap reduces the dimension of the solution space of the matting problem, and leads the matting algorithms to generate user-desired results.

Although binary segmentation and alpha matting are closely coupled problems, in this survey for image matting we will assume that a rough foreground segmentation is given, thus we mainly focus on how to accurately estimate alpha values for truly mixed pixels. We will however discuss binary segmentation techniques in the context of video matting since they play a more central role in recent video matting systems.

1.3 The Trimap

Without any additional constraints, it is obvious that the total number of valid solutions to Equation (1.1) is infinite. For a trivial solution, one can set all α_zs to be 1 and all F_zs to be identical to I_zs, which simply means the whole image is fully occupied by the foreground. Of course this solution is probably not consistent with what a human being will perceive from the input image. To properly extract semantically meaningful foreground objects, almost all matting approaches start by having the user segment the input image into three regions: definitely foreground R_f, definitely background R_b, and unknown R_u. This three-level pixel map is often referred to as a *trimap*. The matting problem is thus reduced to estimating F, B, and α for pixels in the unknown region based on known foreground and background regions. An example of a trimap is shown in Figure 1.1.

Instead of requiring a carefully specified trimap, some recently proposed matting approaches allow the user to specify a few foreground and background scribbles as user input to extract a matte. This intrinsically defines a very coarse trimap by marking the majority pixels (pixels have not been touched by the user) as unknowns.

One of the important factors effecting the performance of a matting algorithm is how accurate the trimap is. Ideally, the unknown region in the trimap should only cover truly mixed pixels. In other words, the unknown region around the foreground boundary should be as thin

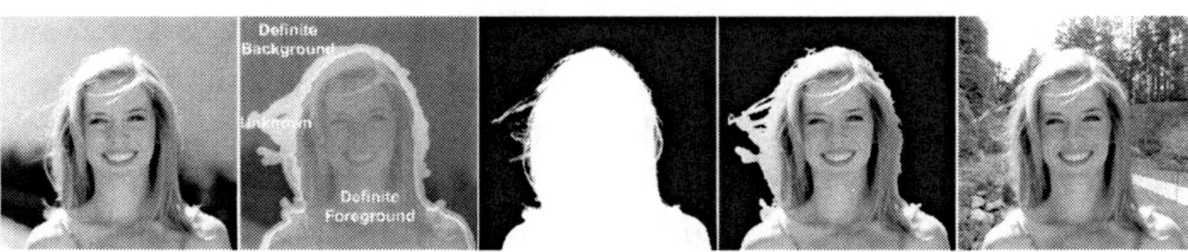

Fig. 1.1 A matting example. From left to right: input image; user specified trimap; extracted matte; estimated foreground colors; a new composite. Results are generated by the Robust Matting algorithm [49].

as possible to achieve the best possible matting results. This is somewhat obvious since the more accurate the trimap is, the less number of unknown variables need to be estimated, and the more known foreground and background information is available to use. However, accurately specifying a trimap requires significant amounts of user effort and is often undesirable in practice, especially for objects with large semi-transparent regions or holes. Thus a big challenge for designing a successful matting algorithm is how to achieve a good trade-off between the accuracy of the matte and the amount of the user effort required. As we will see later, different algorithms have totally different characteristics in this accuracy–efficiency space.

It is worth mentioning that the recently proposed Spectral matting algorithm [22] can automatically extract a matte from an input image without any user input. However, as the authors agreed, the automatic approach has a number of limitations including erroneous results for images with highly textured backgrounds. Thus in practice, user specified trimaps are typically necessary to achieve high quality matting results.

1.4 The User Interface

A properly designed user interface is critical to the success of an interactive system. Surprisingly, although the matting problem has been studied for more than two decades, very little research has been done on exploring good user interfaces for the matting task. Most of the existing matting systems work in an offline mode, where in the interactive loop, the user first specifies a trimap, that invokes matting algorithms to compute a matte. If the result is not satisfactory, the user then refines the trimap and runs the algorithm again. On the other hand, recently proposed matting algorithms mainly focus on how to improve the quality of the matte by introducing more sophisticated analysis and optimization methods, thus they are generally slow. As a result, the interactive loop described above can be very time-consuming and inefficient.

The recently proposed Soft Scissors system [46] demonstrates the possibility of a realtime matting user interface. In this system, a trimap is created incrementally by the user with the aid of a polarized brush stroke (stroke with foreground/background boundary conditions) with dynamically updated parameters. Alpha values of pixels inside the brush stroke are computed in realtime as the user paints along the foreground edge. The instant feedback allows the user to immediately see what the foreground will look like over a new background. This approach opens many new possibilities for creating more efficient and intelligent matting user interfaces.

Another interesting image matting interface is the "components picking" interface proposed in [22]. In this approach a set of fundamental fuzzy matting components are automatically extracted from an input image, based on analyzing the smallest eigenvectors of a suitably defined Laplacian matrix. The user then selects proper components to form the foreground object using simply a few mouse clicks. However, in the case that the automatically computed components are not accurate enough, how to fine adjust the resulting matte on pixel level is unknown. One can imagine combining this approach with other matting interfaces for generating more accurate results.

Designing efficient user interfaces for video matting is certainly a more challenging task. Existing video matting interfaces can be classified into two categories: keyframe-based and volume-based approaches. Systems in the first category allow users to provide inputs on manually or automatically selected keyframes which are sparsely distributed in the input sequence, then try to automatically propagate them into intermediate frames to create a full set of constraints. Volume-based systems treat the video data as a 3D spatio-temporal video cube and allow users to directly marking pixels on extruded surfaces from the 3D cube. Details of these systems will be discussed in Section 6.

1.5 Matting with Extra Information

In early matting systems, the input image is often captured against a single or multiple constant-colored background(s), known as *blue screen matting*. As shown in these approaches, knowing the background greatly reduces the difficulty for extracting an accurate matte.

For better matting results on natural images and video, special imaging systems have been designed to provide additional information or constraints to matting algorithms, such as using flash or non-flash image pairs [39], camera arrays [20], and multiple synchronized video streams [26]. Leveraging these additional sources of information, lower complexity matting algorithms can be designed to achieve fast and accurate matting. These approaches will be discussed in detail in Section 7.

2

Color Sampling Methods for Matting

2.1 Motivation

Although the matting problem is ill-posed, the strong correlation between nearby image pixels can be leveraged to alleviate the difficulties. Statistically, neighboring pixels that have similar colors often have similar matting parameters (i.e., alpha values). This local correlation has been used in many applications such as image denoising, superresolution, colorization, segmentation, etc.

In matting, a straightforward way to use the local correlation is to sample nearby known foreground and background colors for each unknown pixel, I_z. According to the local smoothness assumption on the image statistics, it can be assumed that the colors of these samples are "close" to the true foreground and background colors (F_z and B_z) of I_z, thus these color samples can be further processed to get a good estimation of F_z and B_z. Once F_z and B_z are determined, α_z can be easily calculated from the compositing Equation (1.1).

Although the concept sounds simple, implementing such an algorithm that works well for general images is difficult. There are a number of questions that need to be answered, for instance, how to define the "neighborhood" of pixels. In other words, within what distance can the foreground and background samples be trusted? How many samples should be collected? How can we reliably estimate F_z and B_z from these samples? Existing matting approaches deal with these problems in different ways. Some approaches ignore some of these difficulties by making *ad hoc* assumptions, and some try to solve them in mathematically sound ways. The latter typically results in more accurate and robust matting systems.

2.2 Parametric Sampling Methods

Once foreground and background samples are collected, parametric sampling methods usually fit low order parametric statistical models to them, such as Gaussians. Given an unknown pixel, these models are then used to measure the unknown pixel's "distances" to the foreground and background distributions, which directly leads to its alpha estimation.

2.2.1 Ruzon and Tomasi's Method

An early parametric sampling algorithm was proposed by Ruzon and Tomasi in 2000 [34]. In this approach alpha values are measured along a manifold connecting the "frontiers" of each object's color distribution. As shown in Figure 2.1(a), this approach implicitly assumes that the unknown region is a narrow band around the foreground boundary, and the skeleton of the unknown region can be represented by a chain of pixels. The model construction and alpha estimation procedure is summaried as follows:

(1) Divide the chain of pixels (the skeleton of the unknown region) into intervals by selected *anchor points*.
(2) Centered on each anchor point, define a local spatial window which covers a local unknown region, and a local foreground and background region.
(3) Foreground and background pixels in the local window are used to estimate a foreground and background isotropic

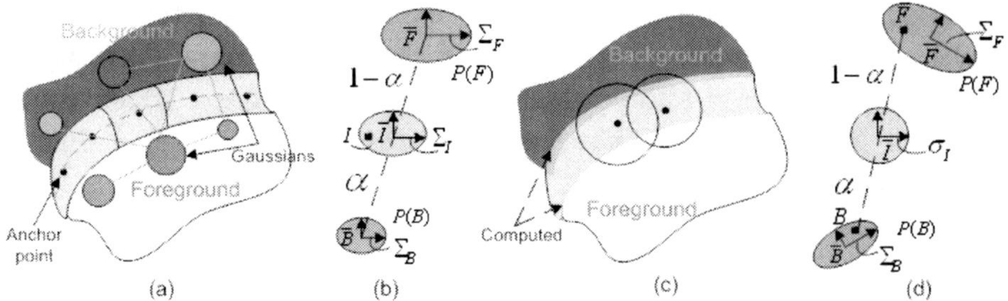

Fig. 2.1 (a) Illustration of the manifold created by Ruzon and Tomasi's Method [34]. (b) Model interpolation in [34]. (c) Neighborhood determined by Bayesian matting [9]. (d) MAP estimation of matte parameters in [9]. The figure is modified from Figure 1 in [9].

(un-oriented) Gaussian distribution, or *point mass*, respectively, in CIE-Lab color space [52].

(4) Build the manifold by collecting foreground Gaussians with background Gaussians, while rejecting some connections according to certain "intersection" and "angle" criteria, as shown as the lines between point masses in Figure 2.1(a).

(5) The observed color of an unknown pixel is modeled as coming from an intermediate distribution between the foreground and background distributions. The intermediate distribution is also defined to be a sum of Gaussians, where each Gaussian has a linearly interpolated mean and covariance between a foreground and background Gaussian pair, according to an estimated alpha value (as shown in Figure 2.1(b)). The optimal alpha is the one that yields an intermediate distribution for which the observed color has maximum probability.

(6) For an unknown pixel, after its alpha value is estimated, its foreground color is estimated by interpolating the means of the foreground and background Gaussian pairs.

From the description above, it is clear that a number of weak assumptions have been made in this approach. The unknown region is assumed to be a narrow band which can be created from dilating a chain a pixels. Selecting anchor points and creating non-overlapping local windows are rather *ad hoc*. Within a local window colors are modeled by non-oriented Gaussians with diagonal covariance matrices, which may generate large fitting errors for textured regions. Also, alpha values are computed independently for unknown pixels, which could result in discontinuities in the final alpha matte.

2.2.2 Bayesian Matting

Based on Ruzon and Tomasi's algorithm, Chuang et al. proposed a Bayesian matting approach in 2001. Similar to Ruzon and Tomasi's algorithm, this approach also models foreground and background colors as mixtures of Gaussians, but with a number of improvements. First, as shown in Figure 2.1(c), Bayesian matting uses a continuously sliding window for neighborhood definition, which marches inward from the foreground and background regions. In addition to the use of foreground and background samples to build color distributions, it also uses nearby computed Fs, Bs, and αs, so that every pixel in the neighborhood will contribute to the foreground and background Gaussians. Furthermore, the matting problem is formulated in a well-defined Bayesian framework and the matte is solved using the maximum *a posteriori* (MAP) technique.

Mathematically, for an unknown pixel I_z, α_z, F_z, and B_z are estimated by

$$\begin{aligned} &\arg\max_{F_z,B_z,\alpha_z} P(F_z,B_z,\alpha_z|I_z) \\ &\quad = \arg\max_{F_z,B_z,\alpha_z} L(I_z|F_z,B_z,\alpha_z) + L(F_z) + L(B_z) + L(\alpha_z), \end{aligned} \quad (2.1)$$

where $L(\cdot)$ is the log likelihood $L(\cdot) = \log P(\cdot)$. The first term is measured as $L(I_z|F_z,B_z,\alpha_z) = -\|I_z - \alpha_z F_z - (1-\alpha_z)B_z\|^2/\sigma_z^2$, where the color variance σ_z is measured locally. This is simply the fitting error according to the compositing Equation (1.1). To estimate $L(F_z)$, foreground colors in the nearby region are first partitioned into groups, and in each group an oriented Gaussian is estimated by computing the mean $\bar{F}$ and covariance Σ_F. $L(F_z)$ is then defined as $-(F_z - \bar{F})^T\Sigma_F^{-1}(F_z - \bar{F})/2$. $L(B_z)$ is calculated in the same way by using background samples. $L(\alpha)$ is treated as a constant.

Equation (2.1) is solved by iteratively estimating F_z, B_z, and α_z using the following steps:

(1) Fix α_z to solve for F_z and B_z as

$$\begin{bmatrix} \Sigma_F^{-1} + I\alpha_z^2/\sigma_z^2 & I\alpha_z(1-\alpha_z)/\sigma_z^2 \\ I\alpha_z(1-\alpha_z)/\sigma_z^2 & \Sigma_B^{-1} + I(1-\alpha_z)^2/\sigma_z^2 \end{bmatrix} \begin{bmatrix} F \\ B \end{bmatrix} = \begin{bmatrix} \Sigma_F^{-1}\bar{F} + I_z\alpha_z/\sigma_z^2 \\ \Sigma_B^{-1}\bar{B} + I_z(1-\alpha_z)/\sigma_z^2 \end{bmatrix}, \tag{2.2}$$

where I is a 3×3 identical matrix.

(2) Fix F_z and B_z to solve for α_z as

$$\alpha_z = \frac{(I_z - B_z)(F_z - B_z)}{\|F - B\|^2}. \tag{2.3}$$

In terms of multiple foreground and background clusters, this process is performed for each pair of foreground and background clusters and the pair which gives the maximum likelihood is chosen.

Bayesian matting can generate accurate mattes when the assumptions are satisfied given an input image and a well-specified trimap. However, once the assumptions are violated, for instance, the input image contains highly textured regions where using Gaussians is insufficient to model the high order statistics of color distribution, or the trimap is coarse so that the correlations between unknown pixels and foreground and background samples are weak, it tends to generate very noisy results, as we will see in Section 5.

2.2.3 Global Color Models

Both Zuron and Tomasi's method and Bayesian matting use local color models by assuming that the unknown region is a narrow band around the foreground boundary, thus there are sufficient foreground and background pixels within a local window centered on any unknown pixel. This assumption will be violated when the user has only provided a very rough trimap using a few paint strokes, where for the majority of unknown pixels, known foreground and background samples are very far away.

Recently a number of systems have been developed to try to estimate good mattes from roughly specified trimaps. To tackle the sampling problem, some of them employ alternative global sampling methods. For instance, the iterative matting approach [48] first trains Gaussian Mixture Models (GMMs) on known foreground and background colors globally, and for an unknown pixel, samples are drawn from all the Gaussians to cover all the possibilities that its foreground color could have. The Geodesic matting approach [3] also uses mixture of Gaussians to model the global foreground and background color distributions in *Luv* space, and fast kernel density estimation methods [53] are used to reduce the computational complexity of constructing the foreground and background Probability Density Functions (PDFs).

2.3 Nonparametric Sampling Methods

Fitting low order statistical models to color samples works well for images containing smooth regions and distinct foreground and background color distributions. However, it will generate large fitting errors when color distributions are significantly non-Gaussian. To avoid this problem, many approaches instead use nonparametric methods to deal with color samples.

2.3.1 Mishima's Method

Mishima [27] developed a blue screen matting technique based on representative foreground and background samples. As shown in Figure 2.2(a), since the background has only one color cluster (blue), all background pixels can be covered by a small sphere approximated by a polyhedra (triangular mesh) in the color space. All foreground pixels form another polyhedra outside the background one. The alpha value of an unknown pixel is then estimated by calculating its relative position to the two polyhedras.

2.3.2 Knockout

The Knockout system [11] first extrapolates foreground and background colors into the unknown region. For an unknown pixel I, its

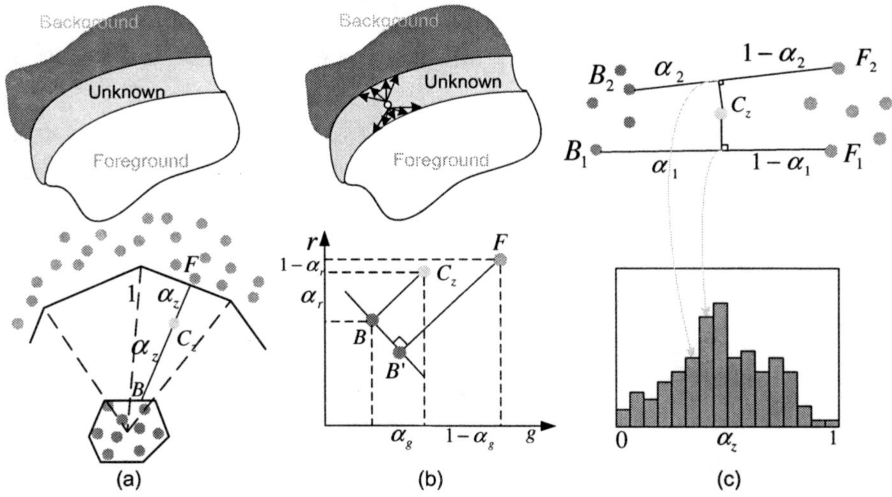

Fig. 2.2 Illustration of nonparametric sampling methods proposed in (a) Mishima's method [27], (b) Knockout [11], and (c) Iterative matting [48]. (a) and (b) are modified from Figure 1 in [9].

foreground color F_z is computed as a weighted sum of nearby known foreground colors, and the weights are proportional to their spatial distances to I. The background color B_z is first calculated in this way as B'_z, then refined by considering the relative position of I and F_z, as shown in Figure 2.2(b). Finally, α_z is estimated three times, each in a color channel. For instance, in red channel the alpha is estimated as $(r(I_z) - r(B_z))/(r(F_z) - r(B_z))$, where $r(\cdot)$ is the red channel value of the color. The final α_z is then estimated as a weighted sum of these values, where the weight is proportional to the foreground and background difference in the corresponding color channel.

2.3.3 Using Histograms

Some matting approaches treat alpha values as random variables, and use foreground and background samples to estimate their underlying PDFs. In the iterative matting system [48], the PDF is approximated as a histogram of discrete alpha levels. The continuous alpha range $[0,1]$ is discretized into k levels, resulting in k possible alpha values $\alpha_1, \ldots, \alpha_K$. For each foreground and background sample pair, all possible values are used to generate synthetic colors. The alpha level which generates a color that is the closest to the unknown pixel is chosen and its bin in the histogram will increase by one.

A histogram can be built in this way by iterating through all sample pairs, for each unknown pixel, as shown in Figure 2.2(c). Mathematically, the likelihood for alpha level α_k is computed as

$$L_k(z) = \frac{1}{N^2} \sum_{i=1}^{N} \sum_{j=1}^{N} w_i^F w_j^B \cdot \exp\big(- d_c(I_z, \hat{I}_z)^2 / 2\sigma_z^{k2} \big), \tag{2.4}$$

where F_i^z and B_j^z are foreground and background samples collected for I_z, $\hat{I}_z$ is the synthetic color computed as $\alpha_k F_i^z + (1 - \alpha_k) B_j^z$, and $d_c(\ )$ is the Euclidian distance function in RGB space. The covariance σ_z^k is computed locally and dynamically as $\alpha_k \sigma_F + (1 - \alpha_k)\sigma_B$, where σ_F and σ_B are covariances of foreground and background samples.

The constructed histograms are then used to support a Belief Propagation algorithm for determining the optimal alpha values that are locally consistent. A similar sampling method is used in the Easy Matting system [17].

2.3.4 Selecting Good Samples

Sampling algorithms described in previous sections typically use all the collected color samplers in a local window. However, when the foreground and background contain complex patterns and/or the input trimap is coarse, the samples may have large color variances, and it is often the case that only a small number of samples are valid to estimate the alpha value for an unknown pixel. To discover which samples from a large sample set are most valid, an optimized color sampling procedure is proposed in [49], which has been later used in the Soft Scissors system [46].

In this algorithm, "good" sample pairs are defined as those that can explain the color of the unknown pixel as convex combinations of themselves. Specifically, as shown in Figure 2.3(b), for a pair of foreground and background colors F^i and B^j, a *distance ratio* $R_d(F^i, B^j)$ is defined to evaluate this sample pair by examining the ratio of the distances between (1) the pixel color, I_z, and the color it would have,

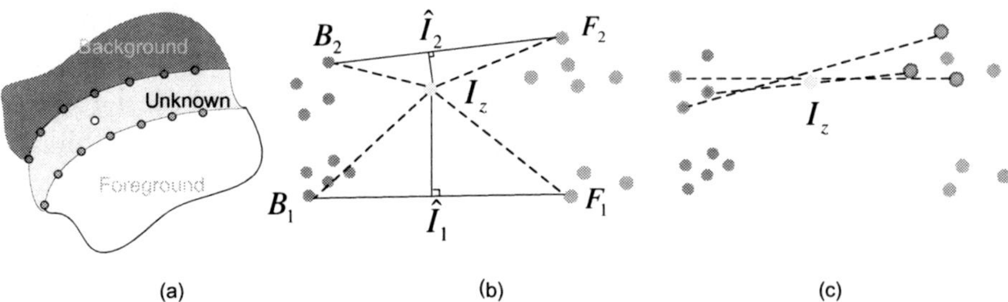

Fig. 2.3 Illustration of the optimized color sampling scheme proposed in [49]. (a) Sparse sample sets construction. (b) Measuring confidence of sample pairs. (c) A small number of best sample pairs are finally chosen.

$\hat{I}$, predicted by the linear model in Equation (1.1), and (2) the distance between the foreground/background pair:

$$R_d(F^i, B^j) = \frac{\|I_z - (\hat{\alpha_z} F^i + (1 - \hat{\alpha_z})B^j)\|}{\|F^i - B^j\|}, \tag{2.5}$$

where $\hat{\alpha_z}$ is computed as Equation (2.3). In the example shown in Figure 2.3(b), the distance ratio will be much higher for pair (F_1, B_1) than pair (F_2, B_2), indicating that the latter is a better choice for estimating the alpha value for I_z.

The distance ratio alone will favor sample pairs that are widely spread in color space since the denominator $\|F^i - B^j\|$ will be large. Since most pixels are expected to be fully foreground or background, pixels with colors that lie nearby in color space to foreground and background samples are more likely to be fully foreground or background themselves. Thus, for each individual sample two more weights $w(F^i)$ and $w(B^j)$ are defined as $w(F^i) = 1.0 - \exp\{-\|F^i - I_z\|^2/D_F^2\}$ and $w(B^j) = 1.0 - \exp\{-\|B^j - I_z\|^2/D_B^2\}$, where D_F and D_B are the minimum distances between foreground/background sample and the current pixel, i.e., $\min_i(\|F^i - I_z\|)$ and $\min_j(\|B^j - I_z\|)$.

Combining these factors, the final *confidence* value $f(F^i, B^j)$ for a sample pair is defined as

$$f(F^i, B^j) = \exp\left\{-\frac{R_d(F^i, B^j)^2 \cdot w(F^i) \cdot w(B^j)}{\sigma^2}\right\}, \tag{2.6}$$

where σ is fixed to be 0.1 in the system.

Every pair of foreground and background samples are examined in this way and finally, as shown in Figure 2.3(c), a small number of pairs with the highest confidences are selected to generate the initial guess of the alpha value for the unknown pixel, which will be further adjusted by an optimization process, as described in Section 4.6.

Since this sampling scheme can deal with relatively large sample sets with high color variances, in [49] a relatively large number of foreground and background pixels are sparsely selected along the boundary of the unknown region to form the sample set, as shown in Figure 2.3(a).

2.4 Summary

Collecting nearby known foreground and background pixels as samples and using them to help estimate alpha values for unknown pixels is a commonly used approach to take advantage of natural image statistics for solving the ill-posed matting problem. As shown in matting approaches described in this section, sampling methods work well when the input image contain smooth regions and the trimap is well-defined. In this case, the correlation between the unknown pixels and known ones are strong and the underlying assumptions of these approaches hold.

As we will show in Section 5, the performance of different approaches varies significantly according to how efficient they use the collected samples. Earlier systems, such as Knockout [11] and Bayesian Matting [9], tend to use all samples equally without considering their legitimacy, thus may introduce significant errors when the sample set is not properly constructed. The recently proposed Robust Matting system [49] presents a sample selection procedure to re-examine the collected samples and only pick out a small number of "good" ones to use, thus can robustly generate more accurate results.

3

Defining Affinities for Matting

3.1 Motivation

As discussed in Section 2, misclassification of color samples in a complex scene is the fundamental limitation for sampling-based approaches. To avoid this problem some recently proposed matting approaches have explored another way of using local image statistics by defining various *affinities* between neighboring pixels, which intrinsically models the *matte gradient* across the image lattice instead of directly estimating the alpha value at each single pixel.

Compared with pure sampling-based approaches, affinity-based approaches have two major advantages. First, affinities are always defined in a small neighborhood, usually between immediately connected pixels or pixels in a 3×3 window. In such a small window, the pixel correlations are usually strong thus the local smoothness assumption typically holds, even for moderately complex images. On the contrary, when the input trimap is coarse, sampling-based approaches are forced to collect samples which are far from the target pixel, thus the samples may or may not be useful at all. On the other hand, the defined affinities regularize the resulting matte to be locally smooth, thus fundamentally avoid matte discontinuities which sampling-based approaches may suffer from.

3.2 Poisson Matting

Poisson matting [38] models the matte gradient by assuming that intensity changes in the foreground and background are locally smooth. Mathematically, an approximate gradient field of the matte is achieved by taking the partial derivatives on both sides of the matting equation (1.1):

$$\nabla I_z = (F_z - B_z)\nabla\alpha_z + \alpha_z\nabla F_z + (1 - \alpha_z)\nabla B_z, \tag{3.1}$$

where $\nabla = (\frac{\partial}{\partial x}, \frac{\partial}{\partial y})$ is the gradient operator. Since F_z and B_z are assumed to be smooth, thus $\alpha_z\nabla F_z + (1 - \alpha_z)\nabla B_z$ is relatively small compared with $(F_z - B_z)\nabla\alpha_z$, and the matte gradient can be approximated as

$$\nabla\alpha_z = \frac{1}{F_z - B_z}\nabla I_z. \tag{3.2}$$

The matte gradient is thus proportional to the image gradient. To estimate the absolute gradient value, $F_z - B_z$ needs to be estimated first. In the system F_z and B_z are simply chosen as the nearest foreground and background colors for the unknown pixel.

The final matte is then constructed by solving Poisson equations on the image lattice as:

$$\alpha^* = \arg\min_{\alpha} \int\int_{z\in\Omega} \left\| \nabla\alpha_z - \frac{1}{F_z - B_z}\nabla I_z \right\|^2 dz \tag{3.3}$$

with the Dirichlet boundary condition which is consistent with the user-provided trimap. Ω is the unknown region in the trimap. Obtaining the unique solution of Poisson equations is a well studied problem and the Gauss–Seidel iteration with over-relaxation method is used in the proposed system.

Formulating the matting problem as solving Poisson equations is technically sound, however, one major limitation of the proposed system is the way $F_z - B_z$s is estimated. For complex scenes, choosing the nearest samples for estimating F_z and B_z will not be accurate, thus could result in large errors in the final solution. To alleviate this problem a set of local filters and operations are defined in the proposed system, which enables the user to manually correct the final matte by solving local Poisson equations. Although good results can be achieved in this way, it is often a time-consuming process for the user.

3.3 Random Walk Matting

A classic affinity defined in many spectral image segmentation approaches [32] is formatted as:

$$w_{ij} = \exp\left(-\frac{\|I_i - I_j\|^2}{\sigma^2}\right), \tag{3.4}$$

where σ is a free parameter which can be either automatically determined or manually set by the user. This affinity was adopted in the Random Walk matting system [16], with the modification that color distances are not measured in the original RGB space, but in the channels created by using Local Preserving Projections (LPP) techniques [18]. The projections defined by the LPP algorithm are given by the solution to the following generalized eigenvector problem:

$$ZLZ^T x = \lambda Z D Z^T x, \tag{3.5}$$

where Z is the $3 \times N$ matrix with each I_i as a column, D is the diagonal matrix defined by $D_{ii} = d_i$ and L is the graph Laplacian matrix given by

$$L_{ij} = \begin{cases} d_i & : \text{ if } \; i = j, \\ -W_{ij} & : \text{ if } i \text{ and } j \text{ are neighbors,} \\ 0 & : \text{ otherwise.} \end{cases} \tag{3.6}$$

Denote the solution to the generalized eigenvector problem of (3.6) by Q, where each eigenvector is a row of Q. The final affinity then is defined as

$$w^*_{ij} = \exp\left(\frac{(I_i - I_j)^T Q^T Q (I_i - I_j)}{\sigma^2}\right). \tag{3.7}$$

In this survey it is shown that LPP-projected RGB values work better than original RGB values in discriminating foreground boundaries from backgrounds. This survey also opens a new window to explore which color space is optimal for the matting task, since most of existing approaches apply their analysis in the RGB space.

A random walk algorithm is employed to calculate the final alpha values based on the affinity. Given an unknown pixel, its alpha value is set to be the probability that a random walker starting from this location will reach a pixel in the foreground before striking a pixel in the background, when biased to avoid crossing the foreground boundary. These probabilities can be calculated exactly by solving a single system of linear equations. Furthermore, a particularly efficient implementation via the graphics processing unit (GPU) is proposed, which is able to solve the matting problem on a 1024×1024 image in about 0.5 seconds (with an accurately defined trimap). This is by far the fastest implementation among existing approaches.

3.4 Geodesic Matting

Instead of calculating the probability that a random walker will reach the foreground first starting from an unknown pixel, the Geodesic Matting approach [3] measures the weighted geodesic distance that a random walker will travel from its origin to reach the foreground. In this approach the geodesic distance computation is linear in time and with minimal memory requirements as well, which allows the system to achieve fast and high-quality segmentation and matting from a few user scribbles, when the affinities between pixels are assigned properly.

Mathematically, the geodesic distance $d(i,z)$ is simply the smallest integral of a weight function over all paths on the image lattice from pixel I_i to the pixel I_z, defined as

$$d(i,z) = \min_{C_{i,z}} \int_0^1 |W \cdot \dot{C}_{i,z}(p)| dp, \tag{3.8}$$

where $C_{i,z}(p)$ is a path connecting the pixels i, z (for $p = 0$ and $p = 1$, respectively). The weights W are set to be the gradient of the likelihood that a pixel belongs to the foreground (resp. background), i.e., $W = \nabla P_F(x)$. To compute this likelihood, user-specified foreground and background pixels are used to train Gaussian Mixture Models using fast kernel density estimation methods [53], resulting in the foreground

PDF $P(x/F)$ and background PDF $P(x/B)$, and $P_F(x)$ is set to be $\frac{P(x|F)}{P(x|F)+P(x|B)}$.

The geodesic distance from an unknown pixel I_z to the foreground is defined as $D_F(z) = \min_{i \in \Omega_F} d(i,z)$, and its distance to the background is defined in the similar way.

Finally, the alpha value is estimated as:

$$\alpha_z = \frac{w_F(z)}{w_F(z) + w_B(z)}, \tag{3.9}$$

where $w_F(z) = D_F(z)^{-r} \cdot P_F(z)$, is the locally adjusted foreground weight. The idea is to combine the geodesic distance $D_F(z)$ with the locally recomputed foreground probability. The parameter r controls the smoothness of the edges. The background weight $w_B(z)$ is computed in the similar way.

The major advantage of this approach is that it is based on weighted distance functions (geodesics), thereby can be solved as a first-order geometric Hamilton–Jacobi equation in computationally optimal linear time. This is particularly favorable for video matting where computational complexity remains to be a serious issue.

The disadvantage of the proposed system is that the weight w in Equation (3.8) is set in a rather simple way, and will not work well when the foreground and background color distributions have large overlaps, where the PDFs $P(x/F)$ and $P(x/B)$ cannot be estimated properly. However, the proposed geodesic-distance-based matting framework is quite general, so that this step could be potentially improved by using more sophisticated discriminant models when dealing with complex scenes.

3.5 Fuzzy Connectedness for Matting

Another matting technique which is similar to the Geodesic matting approach is the newly proposed FuzzyMatte system [54]. Instead of computing geodesic distances from an unknown pixel to known foreground and background regions, it computes the *fuzzy connectedness* (FC) [43] from the unknown pixel to known ones. FC is a concept that effectively captures fuzzy "hanging togetherness" (adjacency and similarity) between image elements. Mathematically, for a pair of adjacent pixel I_1 and I_2, the affinity A^o is defined as:

$$A^o(I_1, I_2) = \lambda\mu(I_1, I_2) + (1 - \lambda)\mu^o_\phi(I_1, I_2), \quad o \in \{f, b\}, \tag{3.10}$$

where μ measures the color similarity between the two pixels, and μ^o_ϕ measures the pixel-scribble similarity which is defined among the colors of p_1 and p_2, and the colors of pixels under the user-specified scribbles. It is essentially defined in the same way as the W parameter in Equation (3.8) in the Geodesic matting approach, by using Gaussian Mixture Models to fit known foreground and background pixels and compute foreground and background PDEs. λ balances the two similarity measures and is between 0 and 1.

The fuzzy connectedness between any two pixels I_i and I_z is defined as:

$$FC^o(i, z) = \max_{C_{i,z}} \left\{ \min_{p=2,\ldots,n} A^o\left(C_{i,z}(p-1), C_{i,z}(p)\right) \right\}, \tag{3.11}$$

where $C_{i,z}(p)$ again is a path connecting the pixels I_i and I_z. Intuitively, the strength of a path between two pixels is defined as the weakest link between two neighboring pixels along the path, and the final fuzzy connectedness is defined as the strength of the strongest path between the two pixels. Compared with the Geodesic distance defined in Equation (3.8), the main difference is to use the minimal link strength within a path instead of integrating all link strengths over the path. This is sometimes preferable for capturing long skinny fuzzy structures. Imagine a fractional pixel which is very close to the known background boundary but far away from the foreground boundary. Using geodesic distance the pixel might be misclassified as background since the paths to the background boundary are significantly shorter than the paths to the foreground boundary, leading to a much smaller geodesic distance to the background. Using fuzzy connectedness this would not happen, since the absolute path length is not considered in this approach. However, one can also imagine that the fuzzy connectedness is more sensitive to image noise, and not as stable as the geodesic distance for complex images where color PDEs cannot be well estimated.

Another contribution made in this approach is that the alpha matte is estimated in an incremental fashion. Whenever a new scribble is added by the user, instead of re-computing the fuzzy connectedness for every unknown pixel, only a small subset of pixels whose fuzzy connectedness need to be updated are selected for re-estimation, thus the final matte can be updated in nearly realtime. This is in spirit similar to the update region solver proposed in the Soft Scissors system [46].

3.6 Closed-form Matting

Both Poisson matting and Geodesic matting approaches involve estimating foreground and background colors/distributions to some extent, which may significantly lower their performance when the estimations are not accurate. The recently proposed Closed-form matting approach [21] avoids this limitation by explicitly deriving a cost function from local smoothness assumptions on foreground and background colors F and B, and show that in the resulting expression it is possible to analytically eliminate F and B, yielding a quadratic cost function in α, which can be easily solved as a sparse linear system of equations.

The underlying assumption made in this approach is that each F and B is a linear mixture of two colors over a small window (typically 3×3 or 5×5) around each pixel, which is referred to as the *color line model.* It is shown that under this assumption, alpha values in a small window w can be expressed as

$$\alpha_i = \sum_c a^c I_i^c + b, \forall i \in w, \tag{3.12}$$

where c refers to color channels, and a^c and b are constants in the window. The matting cost function is then defined as

$$J(\alpha, a, b) = \sum_{j \in I} \left(\sum_{i \in w_j} \left(\alpha_i - \sum_c a_j^c I_i^c - b_j \right)^2 + \epsilon \sum_c a_j^{c2} \right). \tag{3.13}$$

Furthermore, a^c and b can be eliminated from the cost function, yielding a quadratic cost in the α alone:

$$J(\alpha) = \alpha^T L \alpha, \tag{3.14}$$

where L is an $N \times N$ matrix, whose (i,j)th element is

$$\sum_{k|(i,j)\in w_k} \left(\delta_{ij} - \frac{1}{|w_k|}\left(1 + (I_i - \mu_k)\left(\Sigma_k + \frac{\varepsilon}{|w_k|} I_3\right)^{-1} (I_j - \mu_k)\right)\right), \tag{3.15}$$

where Σ_k is a 3×3 covariance matrix, μ_k is a 3×1 mean vector of the colors in a window w_k, and I_3 is the 3×3 identity matrix.

The matrix L, which is called *matting Laplacian*, is the most important analytic result from this approach. The optimal alpha values are then computed as

$$\alpha = \arg\min \alpha^T L \alpha, \quad \text{s.t. } \alpha_i = 1 \text{ or } 0, \quad \forall i \in \partial\Omega, \tag{3.16}$$

which is essentially a problem of minimizing a quadratic error score, thus can be solved by one of the linear system solvers which will be discussed in Section 4.3.3.

The affinity defined in Equation (3.15) and the one defined in Equation (3.4) share the same property that nearby pixels with similar colors have high affinity values, while nearby pixels with different colors have small affinity values. However, the matting affinity in Equation (3.15) does not have a global scaling parameter σ and instead uses local estimates of means and variances. As a result, this localized adaptive setting leads to a significant improvement in performance, as demonstrated in [21].

3.7 Spectral Matting

Further analysis has been conducted on the proposed matting Laplacian in Equation (3.15), resulting in an automatic matting approach called *Spectral matting* [22]. This is the only approach that tries to pull out a foreground matte in a completely automatic fashion.

In this approach the input image is modeled as a convex combination of K image layers as

$$I_z = \sum_{k=1}^{K} \alpha_z^k F_z^k, \tag{3.17}$$

where F_z^k is the kth matting component of the image. The most important conclusion from this approach is that the smallest eigenvectors of the matting Laplacian L span the individual matting components of the image, thus recovering the matting components of the image is equivalent to finding a linear transformation of the eigenvectors. Detailed steps are as follows:

(1) Compute the eigenvectors of L as $E = [e^1, \ldots, e^K]$, so E is a $N \times K$ matrix (N is the total number of pixels).
(2) Initialize α^k by applying a k-means algorithm on the smallest eigenvectors, and project the indicator vectors of the resulting clusters onto the span of the eigenvectors E:

$$\alpha^k = EE^T m^{c^k}. \tag{3.18}$$

(3) Compute matting components by minimizing an energy function defined as

$$\sum_{z,k} |\alpha_z^k|^\gamma + |1 - \alpha_z^k|^\gamma, \quad \text{where } \alpha^k = Ey^k; \tag{3.19}$$

subject to $\sum_k \alpha_z^k = 1$, using Newton's method [12]. γ is chosen to be 0.9 for a robust measure.
(4) Group components into final foreground matte by testing various combinations of matting components and computing the corresponding cost as $J(\alpha) = \alpha^T L \alpha$. To do this more efficiently the correlations between the matting components via L are pre-computed as

$$\Phi(k,l) = \alpha^{k^T} L \alpha^l, \tag{3.20}$$

and the matting cost can be computed as $J(\alpha) = b^T \Phi b$, where b is a K-dimensional binary vector indicating the selected components.
(5) When user's input is provided, the grouping process can take advantage of it by solving a graph-labeling problem using the min-cut algorithm. Details can be found in [23].

The spectral matting approach derives an analogy between hard spectral image segmentation and image matting, and thus provides a very interesting theoretical result. This work is a milestone in theoretic matting research. However, in practice, this approach is limited to images that consist of a modest number of visually distinct components, as pointed out by the authors. For these images, many other approaches can be used to generate higher quality mattes, although more user input is required. Furthermore, given the fact that the size of E is $N \times K$, the memory consumption of this approach is extremely high, and the practical application range of this approach is thus limited.

3.8 Summary

Defining affinities for matting has been proven to be more robust than sampling-based approaches when dealing with complex images. The reason is that affinities are defined only in local windows, thus their underlying assumptions typically hold even for moderately difficult images.

Depending on the underlying assumptions and how the affinity is mathematically defined, the performance of different algorithms varies dramatically. Poisson matting makes weak assumptions on foreground and background colors, thus will introduce significant errors when dealing with complex scenes, as shown later in Section 5. The closed-form matting derives the affinity by conducting very insightful analysis on the theoretic aspects of the matting problem, thus has significantly higher performance than other affinity-based approaches.

There are two possible drawbacks of affinity-based approaches. First, unlike sampling-based approaches, affinity-based techniques focus on first estimating alpha values, and only then estimate foreground colors for unknown pixels based on pre-computed alphas, rather than estimating them jointly for an optimal solution. Second, the alpha matte is estimated in a propagation fashion, from known pixels to unknown ones, thus small errors could be propagated and accumulated to produce more significant errors. As a result, mattes generated by affinity-based approaches are sometimes less accurate than those generated by sampling-based approaches. Detailed comparisons will be shown in Section 5.

4

Optimization by Combining Sampling and Affinities

4.1 Motivation

In many optimization-based computer vision and graphics systems [1, 24, 32], the energy functions to be minimized take the form of a "Gibbs" energy, defined by two terms:

$$E(\underline{l}, \underline{\theta}, z) = U(\underline{l}, \underline{\theta}, z) + V(\underline{l}, z), \tag{4.1}$$

where $\underline{l}$ stands for the "labels" that will be assigned to pixels, and $\underline{\theta}$ is a model that measures the fitness of $\underline{l}$ given z. The first term on the right side is called a *data term*, or *data cost*, which represents the semantic goal of the optimization. In the foreground segmentation problem, this term might enforce, for example, that pixels whose colors are closer to the known foreground colors and further away from background colors to be classified as foreground. The second term is a *neighborhood term*, or *neighborhood cost*, which encourages coherent decisions to be made within local image regions, reflecting a tendency for the solidity of objects. Once the energy function is defined, a variety of optimization tools can be employed to minimize it, analytically or approximately.

This methodology has been recently applied for the matting task. Intuitively, the sampling techniques discussed in Section 2 are capable of analyzing the distances between an unknown pixel to known foreground and background colors, thus they can be used to assign data costs to pixels as the semantic constraint. The affinities defined in Section 3 represent the relationships between nearby pixels, thus they can be employed to set neighborhood costs for neighboring pixel pairs. By combining sampling methods and affinities together in a single optimization process, one can expect more accurate and robust matting solutions.

4.2 Non-closed-form Optimization

The iterative matting approach [48] estimates foreground mattes from a sparse set of user input such as a few foreground and background scribbles. To achieve this an iterative optimization process is employed, where the alpha values are gradually propagated from known pixels to unknown ones, in a front propagation fashion. The matte is modeled as a Markov Random Filed (MRF), and in each iteration the energy function to be minimized is defined as

$$E = \sum_{z \in \psi} E_d(\alpha_z) + \lambda \cdot \sum_{z,v \in \psi} E_s(\alpha_z, \alpha_v). \tag{4.2}$$

The data cost, $E_d(\alpha_z)$, is constructed using the histogram-based sampling method described in Section 2.3.3, where alpha is discretized into K levels and a histogram is built for each unknown pixel as in Equation (2.4). The data cost is then defined for each of the possible states α_z^k as

$$E_d(\alpha_z^k) = 1 - \frac{L_k(z)}{\sum_{k=1}^{K} L_k(z)}. \tag{4.3}$$

The likelihood terms, L, describe how well the estimated alpha value α_z^k, and foreground and background samples for z fit with the actual color I_z, preferring those which generate smaller fitting errors.

The neighborhood cost $E_s(\alpha_z, \alpha_v)$ is defined by using the classic affinity in Equation (3.4), as

$$E_s(\alpha_z, \alpha_v) = 1 - \exp\left(-(\alpha_z - \alpha_v)/\sigma_s^2\right), \tag{4.4}$$

where σ_s is set to be 0.2 empirically.

With the MRF defined above, finding a labeling (α level for each pixel) with minimum energy corresponds to the MAP estimation problem, which are solved by using the loopy Belief Propagation (BP) algorithm [51].

This approach opens a new window for matting research to explore ways to significantly reduce user efforts that are traditionally required for creating accurate trimaps, especially for images with large portions of semi-transparent foreground where the trimap is difficult to create even manually. However, it also presents two major limitations. The global color sampling scheme is used to guide the matte propagation, thus it requires the foreground and background to have distinct, well-separable color distributions. Furthermore, the expensive nonlinear BP optimization process is employed multiple times to create a matte, which might converge to different local minima. The required processing time of this approach is usually very long, which is undesirable in an interactive setting.

4.3 Closed-form Optimization

Newly proposed optimization-based matting approaches, such as the Easy Matting system [17] and the Robust Matting system [49], employ faster closed-form optimization techniques.

4.3.1 Easy Matting

In the easy matting system [17], the energy function to be minimized is defined as:

$$E = \sum_{z \in \psi} \left(\frac{1}{N^2} \sum_{i=1}^{N} \sum_{j=1}^{N} \frac{\|I_z - \hat{I}_z\|^2}{\sigma_z^2} + \lambda \sum_{z \in \mathcal{N}(z)} \frac{(\alpha_z - \alpha_v)^2}{\|I_z - I_v\|} \right). \qquad (4.5)$$

where N is the number of pixels, $\mathcal{N}(z)$, defines a neighborhood around z, and $\hat{I}_z$ is the estimated color given alpha. Both the data term and the neighborhood term are designed in a similar way as in the iterative matting approach [48], except that no exponential mappings are employed. This greatly simplifies the optimization process since Equation (4.5) is a quadratic function, thus the energy can be easily minimized by solving a set of linear equations by using the conjugate gradient method.

Another improvement made in this approach over previous ones is that the weight λ in Equation (4.5) is dynamically adjusted rather than manually fixed, as

$$\lambda = e^{-(k-\beta)^3}, \tag{4.6}$$

where k is the iteration count, and β is a pre-defined constant which is set to be 3.4 in the system. This is motivated by the fact that users often place scribbles inside foreground and background regions, thus a larger λ value, which indicates an emphasis on the neighborhood term, will encourage the foreground and background regions to smoothly spread out in early iterations. Later on when the foreground and background regions encounter at the object boundary where discontinuity presents, the iteration count has increased so that λ will be small, thus the data term will play a more important role to try to estimate accurate alpha values. This dynamic weight setting helps the iterative algorithm avoid stepping into bad local minima in early stages.

4.3.2 Robust Matting

The Robust Matting system [49] combines the optimized color sampling scheme described in Section 2.3.4 and the matting affinity defined in Section 3.6, resulting in a well-balanced system which is capable of generating high quality results while maintaining a reasonable degree of robustness against different user inputs. The energy function to be minimized in this approach, although not explicitly formulated in [49], is defined as

$$E = \sum_{z \in \psi} \left[\hat{f}_z(\alpha_z - \hat{\alpha_z})^2 + (1 - \hat{f}_z)(\alpha_z - \delta(\hat{\alpha_z} > 0.5))^2 \right] + \lambda \cdot J(\alpha, a, b), \tag{4.7}$$

where $\hat{\alpha_z}$ and $\hat{f}_z$ are estimated alpha and confidence values in the color sampling step as described in Section 2.3.4, and $J(\alpha, a, b)$ is the neighborhood energy defined in Equation (3.13), where the parameters a and b can be analytically eliminated in the optimization process.

In [49], minimizing the energy function defined in Equation (4.7) is interpreted as solving a corresponding graph labeling problem as

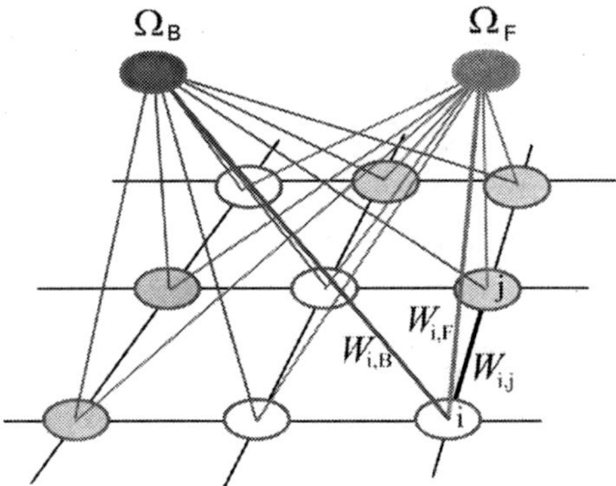

Fig. 4.1 Matting is formulated as solving a soft graph labeling problem in the Robust Matting system [49]. This figure is modified from Figure 6 in [49].

shown in Figure 4.1, where Ω_F and Ω_B are virtual nodes representing pure foreground and pure background, white nodes represent unknown pixels on the image lattice, and light red and light blue nodes are known pixels marked by the user. A data weight is defined between each pixel and a virtual node to enforce the data constraint (the first term on the right side of Equation (4.7)), and an edge weight is defined between two neighboring pixels to enforce the neighborhood constraint (the second term on the right side of Equation (4.7)).

Numerically, similar to the Closed-form matting approach [21], the energy to be minimized is defined as a quadratic function in α_z, thus can be solved using a linear system solver. The Laplacian matrix in the linear system is defined as

$$L_{ij} = \begin{cases} W_{ii} & : \text{ if } \quad i = j, \\ -W_{ij} & : \text{ if } i \text{ and } j \text{ are neighbors,} \\ 0 & : \text{ otherwise,} \end{cases} \tag{4.8}$$

where $W_{ii} = \sum_j W_{ij}$. L is thus a sparse, symmetric, positive-definite matrix with dimension $N \times N$, where N is the number of all nodes in the graph, including all pixels in the image plus two virtual nodes Ω_B and Ω_F. W_{ij} is exactly the same as the one defined in Equation (3.15) if i and j are neighboring pixels; otherwise W_{ij} equals to the data cost $W_{i,F}$ or $W_{i,B}$ if j is a virtual node.

Note that the confidence value $\hat{f}_z$ plays an important role in balancing the data cost and neighborhood cost in Equation (4.7). This is motivated by the fact that color sampling will not be always reliable for every single pixel and bad estimations are typically associated with low confidence values, thus using the confidence value to tone down incorrect data costs and let neighborhood costs take over for those pixels will produce better mattes with less noise.

4.3.3 Linear System Solvers

After reviewing various matting approaches described in Sections 3 and 4, one may have noticed that in a number of affinity-involved matting approaches the energy functions to be minimized are defined in a quadratic form, leading to large linear systems which can be solved by a variety of linear solvers. Such approaches include Poisson matting (Section 3.2), Random Walk matting (Section 3.3), Closed-form matting (Section 3.6), Easy matting (Section 4.3.1), and Robust matting (Section 4.3.2). Note that although these approaches share the same optimization framework, the underlying energy functions are quite different from each other.

Once a linear system is constructed, many existing linear solvers can be applied to solve for the final alpha matte. These solvers can be divided into two categories: direct methods and iterative ones. Direct methods use sparse matrix representations together with stable factorization algorithms such as LU (lower–upper) or Cholesky decomposition to obtain sparse symmetric factor matrices for which forward and backward substitution can be efficiently performed [13]. However, these methods become inefficient for large multi-dimensional problems because of excessive amounts of fill-in that occurs during the solution. Iterative relaxation algorithms use a series of steps that successively refine the solution to minimize the quadratic energy function [35]. Representative techniques include gradient descent, successive over-relaxation (SOR), and conjugate gradient descent. Compared with direct methods they are often more computationally efficient for large scale linear systems.

The basic iterative methods often can be accelerated by techniques such as multigrid, hierarchical basis preconditioning, and tree-based preconditioning. Multigrid methods [7] operate on a pyramid and alternate between solving the problem on the fine level and projecting the error to a coarser level where the lower-frequency components can be reduced. Preconditioning techniques [40, 41] use the multi-level hierarchy to precondition the original system, i.e., to make the search directions more independent and better scaled. The recently proposed locally adapted hierarchical basis functions [41] have been shown to be very effective for preconditioning large optimization problems that arise in computer graphics applications such as tone mapping, gradient-domain blending, and colorization. However, it may not be able to be directly applied to certain matting affinities such as the one defined in [21], due to its limitation on the order of the smoothness terms (only first-order smoothness terms are supported). Details of this technique along with a good survey of related work can be found in [41].

There are also many existing software packages that one can directly use to solve linear matting systems. A straightforward choice is the "backslash" operator in Matlab, or other equivalent Matlab-based linear solver. A good overview of a variety of iterative linear system solver packages can be found in [14].

4.4 Summary

Sampling-based methods and affinity-based approaches both have their own advantages and disadvantages. Sampling-based methods work better when dealing with distinct foreground and background color distributions along with carefully specified trimaps, but tend to generate significant errors when their underlying assumptions are violated. On the other hand, affinity-based approaches are relatively insensitive to different user inputs and always generate smooth mattes. However, they may not be very accurate for long and furry foreground structures. By combining these two methodologies together through an optimization process, more advanced systems can be developed, achieving a good trade-off between accuracy and robustness. The recently proposed Robust Matting system [49] is an example of such a system.

5

Performance Evaluation

5.1 Introduction

Early matting systems often justify their approaches by presenting a few good examples, and rely on the users to visually examine mattes generated by different algorithms for quality assessment. These comparisons thus are often subjective and/or incomplete.

Given the increasing interest in the matting problem from both industry and academia, there is a demand for conducting objective and quantitative comparisons among different algorithms, especially those that have been recently proposed. Such a comparison will reveal strengths as well as weaknesses of different methods, providing promising directions to follow for future research. Furthermore, since no single algorithm can work well in all cases, such an evaluation will help users choose proper methods that can best solve their specific problems.

This issue has been addressed in some recently proposed matting approaches [21, 49], where independent objective evaluations have been conducted, however on totally different data sets. In this survey, a new test data set is constructed by combining various examples used in previous approaches together. The data set is then used for an objective comparison among different algorithms. The methodology used for comparison in this survey is extended from the study conducted in [49].

5.2 The Data Set

The test set includes 6 test images along with ground-truth mattes, as shown in Figure 5.1. Specifically, images T1–T3 are part of the data set constructed in [49], while images T4–T6 have been used in [22] as test examples. All ground-truth mattes are extracted using blue screen matting techniques described in [37]. Specifically, as shown in Figure 5.2, a fuzzy foreground is shot against two known backgrounds, triangulation matting techniques thus can be applied to pull out a fairly accurate matte. For T1–T3, the mattes are then used to create new composites which serve as the test images. For T4–T6, since the foregrounds are shot against a computer screen, the test images are directly captured without re-compositing.

To apply matting algorithms on this data set, a series of user-specified trimaps are also provided for each test example, as shown in Figure 5.2. First, for a test image, a fairly accurate trimap T_0 is manually created. The unknown region of T_0 is then dilated gradually to create a series of less accurate trimaps $T_1, T_2, \ldots, T_9$. The idea is that by applying the same algorithm using different trimaps on the same example, one can examine how sensitive the algorithm is to different user inputs.

Given the fact that some algorithms have the extra ability to work from less user input, such as a few scribbles, for each example we

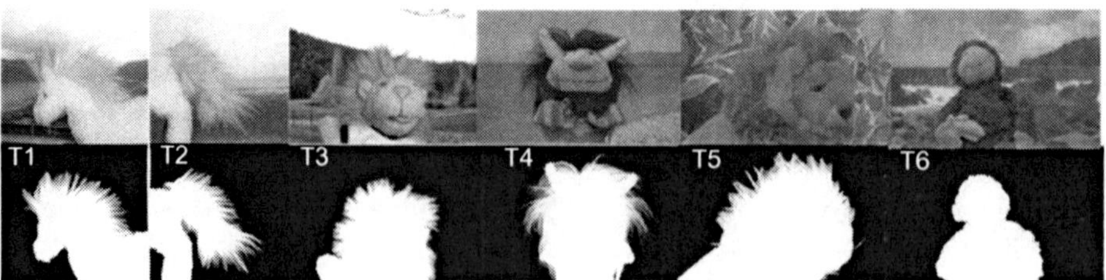

Fig. 5.1 Test images and corresponding ground-truth mattes. Images T1–T3 are from [49], T4–T6 are from [22].

Fig. 5.2 Top: shooting the foreground against two known backgrounds to extract the ground-truth matte and create a new composite. Bottom: fine-to-coarse trimaps. This figured is modified from Figure 8 in [49].

develop an additional set of trimaps based on scribbles, as shown in Figure 5.2, and use them to conduct comparisons among these algorithms.

It is obvious that six test images are not able to cover all possible situations one may expect in real applications, thus the data set is limited in scale. In the newly proposed high resolution matting system [31], a new high-resolution matting ground-truth data set has been constructed, which can be used for more extensive studies in the future.

5.3 Quantitative Measurements

All the computation in our test is conducted on a Dell Precision 690 workstation, with an Intel Xeon 5160 CPU at 3.00 GHz and 4 GB of RAM. Different algorithms are compared in three aspects: *accuracy, robustness, and efficiency.*

Each algorithm is applied to each test image using the pre-defined series of trimaps, resulting a series of mattes. These mattes are then compared to the ground-truth and errors are computed in the Mean Squared Error (MSE) sense as $\{e_1, e_2, \ldots, e_n\}$. The minimal MSE value $\min(e_i)$ is then chosen as the measurement of accuracy, as it is associated with the most accurate matte the algorithm can achieve no matter how much user input it takes.

The maximum MSE value $\max(e_i)$ is used to measure the robustness of the algorithm against different user inputs.

The efficiency of an algorithm is measured as the computational time and memory it takes on each example. These two are hard to measure in a fully objective way since they are closely related to the computational environment. Also, most of the test systems are developed only for research purposes and have not been fully optimized in terms of efficiency. Furthermore, as mentioned in Section 4.3.3, some of the approaches involve solving large linear systems, which could be significantly accelerated by using faster linear solvers. For all these reasons, time and memory cost presented in this study should not be treated as accurate measurement, but rather as reference information to be used to help users choose a proper method to meet their specific computational constraints.

Note that each algorithm may have a set of tunable parameters which may largely affect its performance on a specific example. In this study to ensure a fair comparison, all the parameters are set to be their default values for all algorithms.

5.4 Test Algorithms

We compare the performance of 9 algorithms: Bayesian matting [9], Knockout 2 [11], Iterative matting [48], Global Poisson matting [38], Random Walk matting [16], Robust matting [49], Closed-form matting [21], Easy matting [17], and Geodesic matting [3]. As described in previous sections, these systems can be classified into three categories: sampling-based methods, affinity-based methods, and approaches combining sampling with affinity, as shown in Table 5.1. These algorithms form a representative ensemble of existing image matting approaches.

5.5 Comparisons on Trimaps

In the first round of test, all algorithms are applied with the series of trimaps T_0–T_9. Comparisons on scribble-based input will be presented

Table 5.1 Matting algorithms tested in this study.

	Sampling-based	Affinity-based	Combined
Bayesian [9]	•		
Knockout2 [11]	•		
Random Walk [16]		•	
Poisson [38]		•	
Closed-form [21]		•	
Iterative [48]			•
EasyMatting [17]			•
Robust [49]			•
Geodesic [3]			•

later. The geodesic matting approach is not included in the trimap-based test since it is primarily designed for scribble-based input as an efficient method for generating trimaps, as described in [3].

5.5.1 Accuracy and Robustness

Figure 5.3 shows the MSE curves of different algorithms for test image $T2$. As expected, most algorithms achieve their best performance on the finest trimap. As the trimap becomes coarser, their performances generally degrade, but at different rates. Partial mattes are shown at two trimap levels (2 and 8) since MSE values do not precisely represent visual quality.

Table 5.2 shows the Minimal MSE values as the measure of accuracy for all algorithms on the data set along with their ranks. Table 5.3 shows the Maximum MSE values as the measure of robustness for all algorithms on the data set along with their ranks.

This study reveals that pure sampling-based approaches usually work well with fine trimaps, but as the trimap becomes coarser, their performance degrades dramatically. For instance, the maximum MSE of Bayesian matting on example T3 is 7.34 times larger than the minimal MSE it achieves with the finest trimap, indicating that this approach is very sensitive to user input. This conclusion is consistent with the theoretic analysis conducted in Section 2.

Pure affinity-based approaches generate more stable results in the test. For instance, the maximum MSE of Closed-form matting on example T3 is only 31.1% larger than the minimal MSE it achieves, indicating its robustness against different user inputs. This observation again is

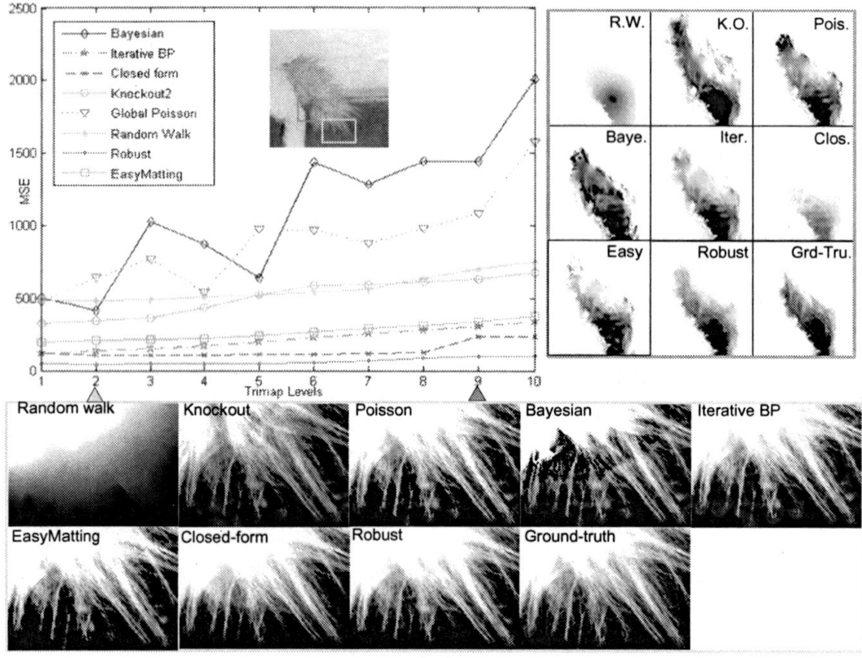

Fig. 5.3 Top left: MSE curves for test image T2. Top right and bottom: Partial mattes computed at two trimap levels 2 and 9 (indicated by colored triangular marks).

Table 5.2 Minimal MSE (representing accuracy) of different algorithms and their ranks.

	T1	T2	T3	T4	T5	T6	Rank
Bayesian	453^7	415^6	137^5	282^6	423^6	39^4	5.7
Knockout	155^5	326^5	113^3	157^3	205^3	37^3	3.7
Rand.Walk	286^6	482^8	218^7	581^7	441^7	73^7	7.0
Poisson	717^8	477^7	843^8	1500^8	1099^8	161^8	7.8
Clos.-form	79^3	105^2	61^2	89^1	148^1	36^2	1.8
Iterative	61^2	118^3	130^4	180^4	337^4	43^6	3.8
EasyMatting	127^4	198^4	156^6	228^5	397^5	40^5	4.8
Robust	46^1	44^1	38^1	99^2	179^2	35^1	1.3

Note: Last column shows the average ranks.

consistent with the theoretic analysis conducted in Section 3. Note that some approaches, such as Global Poisson matting and Random Walk matting, cannot achieve very accurate results on this data set, due to their specific weaknesses in defining the affinities as addressed in Section 3.

By combining sampling methods with neighborhood affinities, optimization-based approaches typically achieve a good balance

Table 5.3 Maximal MSE (representing robustness) of different algorithms and their ranks.

	T1	T2	T3	T4	T5	T6	Rank
Bayesian	1198^7	2006^8	1005^7	913^7	1176^7	97^6	7.0
Knockout	321^5	678^5	180^3	297^4	383^2	76^4	3.8
Rand.Walk	343^6	748^6	278^6	643^6	495^5	107^7	6.0
Poisson	1959^8	1577^7	1736^8	3242^8	2511^8	635^8	7.8
Clos.-form	97^2	234^2	80^2	449^5	389^3	59^2	2.7
Iterative	182^3	337^3	205^4	225^1	479^4	84^5	3.3
EasyMatting	270^4	377^4	220^5	252^3	517^6	66^3	4.2
Robust	85^1	101^1	67^1	229^2	363^1	49^1	1.2

Note: Last column shows the average ranks.

between accuracy and robustness. Specifically, the Robust Matting system, which combines the optimized color sampling procedure (Section 2.3.4) and the closed-form matting affinity (Section 3.6) together, constantly ranks the first in terms of both accuracy and robustness.

5.5.2 Efficiency

Table 5.4 shows the approximate processing time of different algorithms, using the level 5 trimap for each example. Note that the Random Walk matting algorithm used in this test is fully implemented on CPU rather than GPU as described in the original paper, so the actual GPU implementation may require significantly less processing time.

Table 5.5 shows the approximate memory requirements for different algorithms on example T4 with the level 5 trimap.

Based on time and memory costs, we label each approach as computationally inexpensive, moderately expensive, or very expensive.

Table 5.4 Processing time on trimap No. 5 (in seconds).

	T1	T2	T3	T4	T5	T6
Bayesian	288	408	84	721	85	6
Knockout	2	2	2	2	2	1
Rand.Walk[a]	2	2	2	3	3	1
Poisson	14	11	9	26	18	4
Clos.-form	4	4	4	7	6	3
Iterative	240	300	173	507	250	66
EasyMatting	5	7	2	14	3	1
Robust	5	7	4	14	6	2

[a]Implemented on CPU rather than GPU.

Table 5.5 Memory consumption on Example T4 with trimap No. 5 (in Mb). The image size is 1008 × 672 with 19.8% unknown pixels.

Bayesian	Knockout	Rand.Walk	Poisson	Clos.-form	Iterative	EasyMatting	Robust
130	10	30	22	45	450	46	48

Specifically, Knockout2 and Random Walk matting are labeled as inexpensive given their low requirements on both time and memory. Poisson Matting, Closed-form matting, Robust Matting, and Easy Matting are labeled as moderately expensive. Bayesian matting and Iterative matting are labeled as very expensive, since both require significantly large amounts of processing time and memory.

5.6 Comparisons on Scribbles

Four approaches are compared by using scribble-based user inputs (at three levels): Closed-form matting, Robust Matting, Geodesic matting, and Geodesic+Robust matting. The last method, introduced in [3], is a hybrid approach which first applies geodesic matting algorithm to generate a trimap, then uses Robust matting algorithm to estimate fine foreground details.

Table 5.6 shows the minimal and maximal MSE values of the four algorithms on the data set along with their ranks. Table 5.7 shows their costs in time and memory on example T4 using the second level scribbles. Figure 5.4 shows partial mattes generated on example T4 using the third level scribbles.

Table 5.6 Minimal and Maximal MSE of different algorithms and their ranks for scribble-based user input (Format: $\min(MSE)^{rank} : \max(MSE)^{rank}$).

	Closed-form	Robust	Geodesic	Geodesic+Robust
T1	$181^2 : 1155^3$	$237^3 : 1674^4$	$377^4 : 385^2$	$138^1 : 217^1$
T2	$275^2 : 1308^3$	$433^3 : 1337^4$	$853^4 : 856^2$	$238^1 : 766^1$
T3	$72^2 : 202^2$	$83^3 : 476^4$	$272^4 : 283^3$	$57^1 : 99^1$
T4	$79^1 : 161^2$	$97^3 : 436^3$	$417^4 : 437^4$	$94^2 : 143^1$
T5	$112^2 : 3555^4$	$142^3 : 2188^3$	$294^4 : 304^2$	$96^1 : 252^1$
T6	$48^2 : 153^3$	$65^4 : 329^4$	$93^3 : 94^2$	$45^1 : 49^1$
Rank	1.8 : 2.8	3.2 : 3.7	3.8 : 2.5	1.2 : 1.0

Note: Bottom line shows the average ranks.

Table 5.7 Time (in second) and memory (in Mb) consumption on Example T4 with scribble set 2(Format: time:memory). The image size is 1008 × 672 with 92.8% unknown pixels.

Closed-form	Robust	Geodesic	Geodesic + Robust
11:48	15:62	1:50	9:70

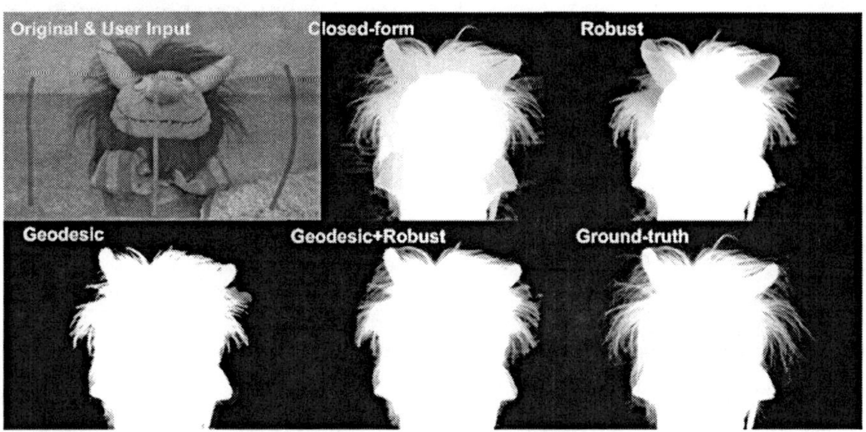

Fig. 5.4 Results of scribble-based matting on example T4.

Geodesic matting stands out in terms of efficiency: it is almost 10 times faster than any other methods, which is not a surprise given the linear complexity of its computation. However, as shown in the results, Geodesic matting alone cannot generate accurate mattes for hairy regions due to the simple color models used for final alpha estimation around foreground boundaries.

The best results are achieved by the hybrid approach, which generates noticeably higher quality mattes than other methods. The computational efficiency of the method is also quite impressive. By combining the advantages of Geodesic segmentation and Robust matting together, it becomes a powerful and practical tool for extracting high quality mattes in an efficient way.

5.7 Accuracy vs. Cost Analysis

Each algorithm presents unique characteristics in our tests. Some approaches are fast to compute but cannot generate accurate mattes,

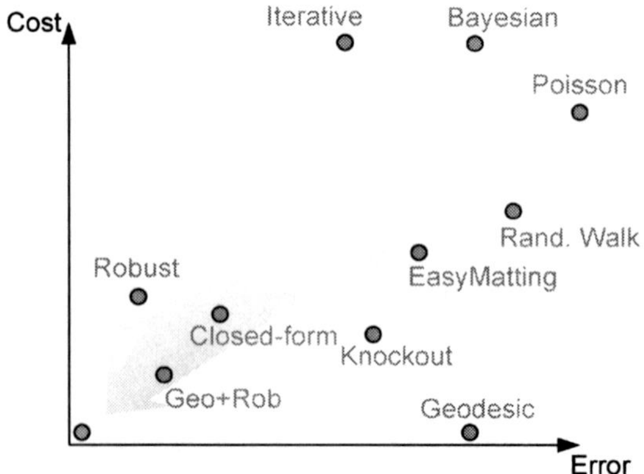

Fig. 5.5 Accuracy vs. Error analysis of existing matting approaches.

and some have the opposite attributes. By jointly considering both accuracy and efficiency, each algorithm can be located in a two dimensional error-cost space, as shown in Figure 5.5. The horizontal axis is error, which measures the degree of accuracy that an algorithm can achieve. The vertical axis is cost, which combines the effort users need to spend on an algorithm to achieve its best possible results, including both labor (how much user input is needed) and computational resources. An ideal (user preferred) matting algorithm should have both small errors and costs, thus is located at the bottom-left corner of the diagram as indicated in red. Recently proposed matting systems are converging in this direction, but there is still considerable room for further improvement, in terms of both accuracy and efficiency.

5.8 Summary

A quantitative and objective evaluation compares the performance of existing matting algorithms, in terms of accuracy, robustness against different user inputs, and computational efficiency. To achieve this a test data set is constructed where each test image is accompanied by a ground-truth matte and a series of predefined trimaps and scribbles as user inputs. Extracted mattes are compared to the ground-truths in the MSE sense as the measure of accuracy and robustness. Computational efficiency is measured by examining the time and memory costs of each algorithm.

Both advantages and disadvantages of each algorithm are revealed and addressed in this study, and are summarized in a single Error vs. Cost figure (Figure 5.5). From the practical stand point of view, an ideal matting algorithm should be able to generate accurate mattes for fairly complicated examples while using the least amounts of user input and computational resources. Recently proposed matting approaches are approaching toward this goal, as shown on the Error vs. Cost figure.

6

Extension to Video

6.1 Introduction

In parallel to image matting research, video matting, the process of pulling a matte from a video sequence of a dynamic foreground element against a natural background, has also received considerable attention. Video matting is a critical operation in commercial television and film production, giving the power to insert new elements seamlessly into a scene, or to transport an actor into a completely new environment in order to create novel visual artifacts.

Extracting foreground objects from still images is a hard problem, as demonstrated in previous sections. Unfortunately, extracting dynamic objects from video sequences is an even more challenging task, although there are also possible advantages. The challenges mainly come from the following aspects:

- *Large data size.* The algorithms must be able to efficiently process the large number of pixels in a video sequence. In particular, the algorithms must be fast enough so that the interface appears responsive and the user remains engaged in the extraction task.

- *Temporal coherence.* It has been proven that human visualization system (HVS) is very sensitive to temporal inconsistencies presented in video sequences [44]. However, applying image matting algorithms naively on per-frame-basis often results in temporal incoherence. How to estimate mattes consistently across frames is one of the biggest challenges for video matting.
- *Fast motion vs. low temporal resolution.* Typical video cameras only capture at 30 frames per second, thus the sampling rate is much lower than ideal when dealing with fast motions. Building correspondence across frames and maintaining temporal coherence in this case is very difficult.

Some advantages can arise in matting objects from videos versus images. If the foreground moves across the background, a more complete background model can be constructed to matte against. Also, the edges between foreground and background can be easier to determine since the texture on the foreground side of the edge remains intact, while the background side of the edge changes as new portions of the background are covered up or revealed.

A number of techniques have been proposed in existing video matting approaches to alleviate the difficulties and leverage the advantages. To deal with large data size, most approaches adopt a two-step framework. In the first step, only binary segmentation is solved to generate a trimap for each frame. Given the trimaps, matting algorithms are then applied in the second step to refine the foreground boundary. Since only binary segmentation is considered in the first step, these approaches can give users rapid response through various user interfaces. Once accurate trimaps are generated, image matting algorithms can then be applied offline on each frame to generate the final fine mattes.

To address the importance of temporal coherence, instead of creating trimaps on video frames independently, most approaches create trimaps in a temporally coherent way, by performing spatio-temporal optimizations. This also allows trimaps to be propagated from a limited number of user defined keyframes to the entire sequence, resulting in significantly reduced user input.

When facing fast motions, most approaches rely on the user to provide dense input as guidance for properly tracking objects across frames. Including users in the loop ensures that the systems are able to handle sequences at a variety of difficulty levels.

6.2 Interpolating Trimaps Using Optical Flow

As a widely used technique for estimating the inter-frame motion at each pixel in a video sequence, optical flow has been used in the Bayesian video matting system [8] for trimap propagation. The basic idea is to ask the user to specify trimaps on a few keyframes in the input sequence, and then use optical flow [5] to propagate trimaps to all other frames.

Unfortunately, optical flow estimation is often erroneous, especially for large motions. To ensure the trimap propagation is stable, a set of supplemental methods have been proposed, as shown in Figure 6.1. In the first step, the system requires the user to specify some "garbage mattes" to eliminate the foreground on some frames. This allows a dynamic clean background plate to be reconstructed from a composite mosaic [42] of the remaining backgrounds in each frame. Both trimap propagation and matte estimation can leverage the constructed background plate.

In the second step, bi-directional (forward and backward) flow is computed to guide the user-specified trimaps from keyframes to intermediate frames. Specifically, from frame t, a forward flow is computed from the previous keyframe t^k to t, along with an accumulated error

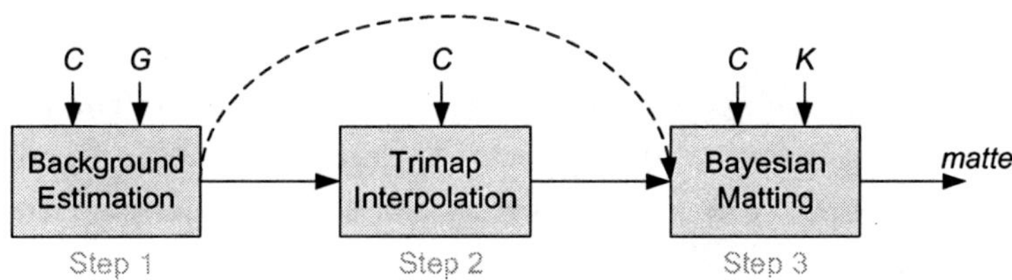

Fig. 6.1 Flowchart of Bayesian video matting system. C is the input sequence, K is user-selected keyframes, and G stands for garbage trimaps. This figure is modified from Figure 1 in [8].

map $E^t_{t^k}$. The trimap M_{t^k} is then warped to frame t as M^f_t. A backward flow from the next key frame t^{k+1} is computed in a similar way, resulting an accumulated error map $E^t_{t^{k+1}}$ and a warped trimap M^b_t. The two warped trimaps are then unified by choosing the assignment with smaller error at each pixel. If the two error maps are large at a particular pixel, the pixel is then either set to be unknown, or to be background if its color is close enough to the color in the background plate computed in the first step.

In the third step, Bayesian matting is applied on each frame with the propagated trimap. The estimated background plate is also used to both improve the quality of the matte and speed up the matting process.

Although optical flow is used in a very conservative way in the system, its performance is still limited by the accuracy of flow estimation, which is often quite erroneous. Furthermore, the background plate estimation assumes that the background undergoes only planar-perspective transformation, which may not be true for sequences in which the background contains moving objects.

6.3 Rotoscoping for Trimap Generation

Another commonly used production matting technique is rotoscoping. In traditional film production, rotoscoping often refers to the process of manually tracing shapes, performed one frame at a time, through a captured image sequence. Recently, optimization techniques have been introduced into rotoscoping process and a keyframe-based rotoscoping system has been proposed [2], which significantly reduces the amount of human effort involved for tracking shapes.

The process starts by having the user select two keyframes t_a and t_b, and draw a set of curves indicating object boundaries on them. Curves are specified by placing control points of a piecewise cubic Bézier curve with C^0 continuity. The curves drawn on t_a can be copied to t_b and modified to fit the new object position.

The system then solves an optimization problem to locate these curves in the intermediate frames. Two types of energy terms are defined in the objective function, *image terms* and *shape terms*.

The image terms prefer curves that closely follow the motion of image features or contours. The shape terms penalize quickly moving and deforming curves. Mathematically the objective function to be minimized is defined as:

$$E = w_V E_V + w_L E_L + w_C E_C + w_I E_I + w_G E_G, \tag{6.1}$$

where $w_{\{V,L,C,I,G\}}$ are pre-defined weights, $E_{\{V,L,C\}}$ are shape terms, and $E_{\{I,G\}}$ are image terms. Specifically, E_V penalizes fast motion, E_L penalizes the change over time of the length of the vector between adjacent samples of a curve, and E_C measures the change in the second derivative of the curve over time. The image term E_I suggests pixels that are close to curves on adjacent frames should have similar colors, and E_G encourages the curves to attach to high gradient points which are typically boundary pixels. The total energy E has the general form of a nonlinear least squares (NLLS) problem, and can be minimized using the well-studied Levenberg–Marquardt (LM) method. Examples of roto curves are shown in Figure 6.2.

Although the rotoscoping system is described as a binary segmentation tool, it can be used to generate trimaps for further accurate boundary matting, by creating a narrow band around the object boundary using the correctly interpolated curves. However, the limitation of this approach lies in the fact that it requires the object to maintain the same topology without occlusion, since valid boundary correspondence

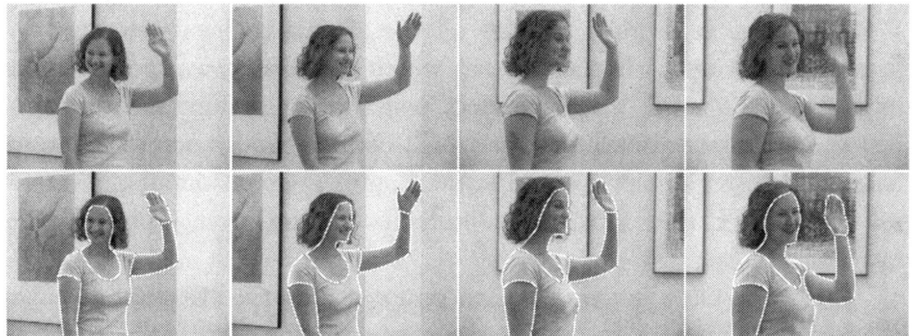

Fig. 6.2 Examples of roto-curves generated in the keyframe-based rotoscoping system [2]. Images are taken from [2].

will not exist when the foreground changes topology or self-occlusions occur. The application range of the keyframe-based rotoscoping system is thus limited to simple motions.

6.4 Graph-Cut Segmentation for Trimap Generation

Graph-cut has been demonstrated to be an efficient optimization tool for interactive image segmentation [6, 24, 32]. Given its promising performance on single images, it is a natural thought to extend it to video sequences for spatio-temporal video object segmentation. Two successful systems, the video object cut-and-paste system [25] and the interactive video cutout system [47], have been independently developed and proposed at the same time based on this idea.

6.4.1 Object-Cut-and-Paste System

There are three main steps in the video object cut-and-paste system [25]: 3D graph-cut segmentation, tracking-based local refinement, and a coherent matting method for generating the final mattes. The first two steps are used to accurately generate trimaps for video frames.

3D graph-cut segmentation: The user first provides accurate foreground segmentation on some keyframes as initial guidance. Between each pair of successive keyframes, a 3D graph $\mathcal{G} = \langle \mathcal{V}, \mathcal{A} \rangle$ is then built on atomic regions (obtained with pre-segmentation using the watershed algorithm [45]) instead of individual pixels, as shown in Figure 6.3. $\mathcal{V}$ is the node set which includes all the atomic regions generated by pre-segmentation. $\mathcal{A}$ is the link set which contains two types of links: intra-frame links $\mathcal{A}_I$ which connect neighboring regions on the same frame, and inter-frame links $\mathcal{A}_T$ which connect nodes across adjacent frames. Two regions on two adjacent frames are considered as temporal neighbors if they have both similar colors and overlapping spatial locations.

The graph-cut algorithm is then performed on the 3D graph to solve the segmentaion/labeling problem. Intuitively, the graph-cut optimization will maintain the color consistency of foreground/background color distributions which are initially constructed based on user-provided

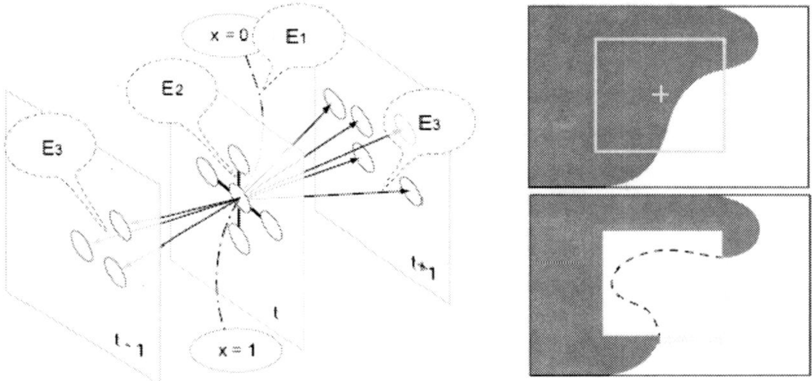

Fig. 6.3 Demonstration of the video object cut-and-paste system [25]. Left: 3D graph cut construction. E_1, E_2, and E_3 are different energy terms defined on different types of links. Right top: Tracked window on one frame. Right bottom: applying local graph-cut segmentation in the tracked window results in a refined segmentation. Illustrations are taken from [25].

segmentation on keyframes, and at the same time maximize the color differences between regions across the object boundary. Gaussian mixture models (GMMs) are used to describe color distributions in the system.

Tracking-based local refinement: Since the foreground/background color distributions are built globally from the keyframes, the graph-cut segmentation may be erroneous in areas where the foreground color matches with the background color at a different part of the video, and vice versa. To solve this problem a tracking-based local refinement algorithm is proposed.

As shown in Figure 6.3, a video tube is interactively constructed, which consists of rectangular windows $\{W_t\}_{t=1}^{T}$ across T frames. This is done by having the user place two key windows W_1 and W_T on two keyframes, and the windows on the intermediate frames are automatically located by a bi-directional feature tracking algorithm. The tracking algorithm is similar in spirit to the rotoscoping algorithm described in the previous section, but is defined on rectangular windows instead of curves. The energy terms defined in this process ensure the video tube to vary smoothly, both in color and location of windows, and also force intermediate windows to capture image patches that are similar to W_1 and W_T.

After tracking is performed, a constrained 2D pixel-level graph-cut segmentation is applied to each window individually using the local foreground and background color models constructed from the windows in the keyframes, as shown in Figure 6.3. Finally, the refined segmentation result in each window is seamlessly connected to the existing boundary outside the window.

Coherent matting: To create the final matte, the binary segmentation boundary is dilated by 10 pixels to create a narrow band as the unknown region for matting. The coherent matting algorithm [36] is used, which improves Bayesian matting by introducing a regularization term for the alpha. Hence, it produces an alpha matte that complies with the prior binary segmentation boundaries, and performs better than Bayesian matting when foreground and background colors are similar.

6.4.2 Interactive Cut-Out System

Another 3D graph-cut based video object cutout system is proposed in [47], where a number of techniques are developed, both in the underlying segmentation algorithms and the user interface. The two main contributions of this work are: (1) a hierarchical graph-cut-based video segmentation algorithm which enables the task of segmenting a 200-frame video sequence to be interactive; and (2) a novel volumetric painting interface which allows the user to easily specify the dynamic spatio-temporal foreground object.

Mean-shift pre-segmentation: A mean-shift clustering algorithm [10] is applied twice to build a strict hierarchical representation of the input video sequence, as shown in Figure 6.4. Pixels are first grouped into 2D spatial regions on each frame using mean-shift image segmentation. The complete collection of 2D regions, parameterized by their mean positions and colors, are then clustered into 3D spatio-temporal regions. This procedure generates a strict hierarchy of regions so that each pixel belongs to a single 2D region and each 2D region belongs to a single

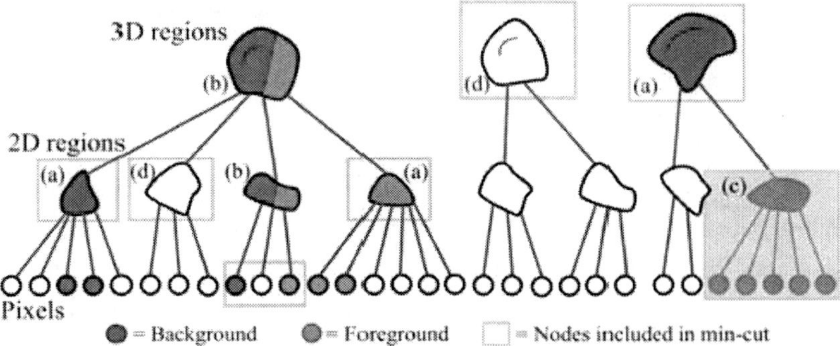

Fig. 6.4 The hierarchical mean-shift structure of a video in [47]. As users mark foreground (red) or background (blue) pixels the labels are propagated up the trees. (a) Nodes that contain only red or blue paint are fully constrained. (b) Mixed nodes are left out of the graph due to conflicting paint strokes in their children. (c) If an entire subtree is marked as background (highlighted in gray) it is removed from further consideration. (d) The graph-cut algorithm must assign a label to each white node in the graph. To apply graph-cut the highest level nodes of a single color (highlighted in yellow) are used for graph construction. This figure is taken from [47].

3D region. The exact coverage ensures that each pixel is given exactly one label in the interactive min-cut optimization.

Once the user has marked some pixels as foreground and some as background, the labels are propagated up the trees in the video hierarchy. The min-cut graph is dynamically constructed each time a segmentation is performed, by using only the highest level nodes that have no label confliction. This is significantly different from other approaches [24, 25, 32] where the graph is constructed once with fixed topology. This dynamic graph construction has two major advantages:

(1) *Fast segmentation.* Since only a small number of nodes are included in the graph, the optimization process can be speed up dramatically. As shown in the examples, a 200-frame 720×480 sequence can be segmented within 10 seconds.
(2) *The ability to correct pre-segmentation errors.* In the system pre-segmentation errors can be corrected by the user by adding paint strokes to the erroneous regions, which will break down higher level nodes into lower level ones. In other words, when pre-segmentation errors are apparent, the user has the ability to force the system to segment the erroneous

regions at a finer resolution, such as the 2D region level, or even at the pixel level.

To achieve a good segmentation using graph-cut optimization, data and link costs must be properly assigned on the constructed graph. In addition to global colors models used in previous approaches [24, 25, 32], a set of local color and edge models are also proposed in the system to leverage the advantages video offers. The local models are combined with the global models to achieve the best possible results.

Volumetric painting interface: A novel interface is developed in the system which allows users to interactively access pixels that lie inside the video volume. As shown in Figure 6.5, the video volume is treated as a 3D cube of data where the X- and Y-axes represent the normal horizontal/vertical axes of a single frame, while the Z-axis represents time. Users can rotate the cube to view it from any angle, cut through the cube with cutting planes at any orientation and slice through parts of the cube by drawing arbitrary surfaces through it. These manipulations make it easy to mark foreground and background pixels within the volume using simple paint strokes as well as larger-scale volume fill operations.

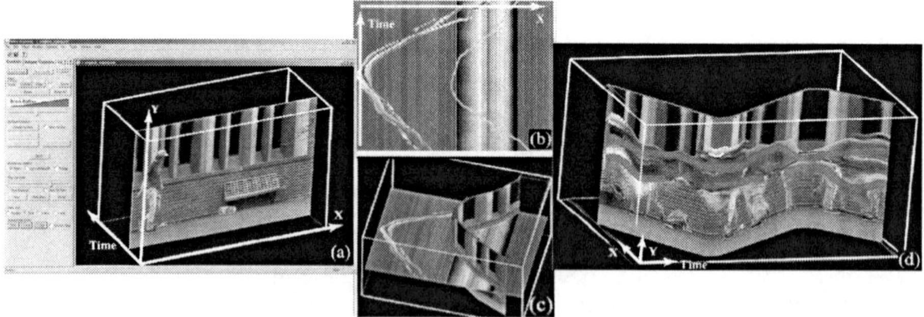

Fig. 6.5 The volumetric painting interface presented in [47]. (a) The user rotates a video volume. (b) An XZ-view of the video volume. The user draws a green curve to extrude a surface through the volume. (c) The extruded surface allows the user to fill the right side of the volume with background paint (blue tint on XZ-plane). (d) Another curve drawn along the foreground's path creates an extruded surface that allows the user to quickly mark the object with red foreground paint across multiple frames. Images are taken from [47].

Spatio-temporal cutting surfaces are very useful for isolating the motion of objects over the entire video sequence in a single image. Figure 6.5(d) shows an extruded surface where the foreground object is spread out over much of the surface. By applying red, foreground paint over the foreground object on this curved surface, the user quickly indicates foreground pixels across many parts of the spatio-temporal volume. Cutting the volume with such surfaces is especially useful for marking thin moving structures that may be difficult to paint in a standard video frame.

Boundary refinement: The foreground boundary generated by binary graph-cut segmentation is typically noisy. To refine the boundary, a pixel-level graph-cut segmentation is performed within a narrow band (usually 10 pixel wide) of the initial boundary. The graph is constructed by treating each pixel within the band as a node, and each node is connected to its immediate spatial/temporal neighbors. A color sampling and modeling algorithm which is similar to the one used in [9] is employed to assign proper data and link costs in the graph.

Finally, a 3D border matting algorithm, improved from the 2D border algorithm proposed in [32], is applied to estimate a spatio-temporally coherent matte for the foreground. The foreground boundary is first parameterized, and boundaries on adjacent frames are then matched using a shape context-based [4] boundary matching algorithm. In this way a consistent 3D contour mesh can be constructed across the entire video volume, which is then used in the border matting algorithm for generating the final matte. Similar to the coherent matting algorithm used in [25], the 3D border matting algorithm also assumes a strong profile for the alpha matte, thus is able to generate stable alpha mattes even if the foreground and background colors are similar.

6.5 Geodesic Segmentation for Trimap Generation

The geodesic segmentation and matting approach [3], which has been described in Section 3.4, has also been extended to video sequences. In this approach video is also modeled as a 3D cube of pixels, in which every pixel has six neighbors, four spatially and two temporally. The user first specifies foreground and background scribbles on some

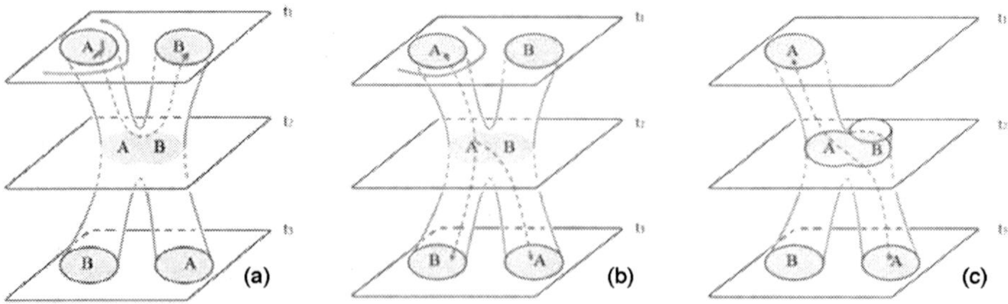

Fig. 6.6 Video tubes used in geodesic video segmentation [3]. (a) Although the scribbles in frame t_1 intend to separate A as foreground, the foreground label (red) reaches the object B by a path in 3D space where both objects A and B overlap. (b) and (c) The scribble propagation is constrained to move forward and the branch between t_1 and t_2 is eliminated. Illustrations are taken from [3].

keyframes, and the scribbles are then propagated throughout the whole video by calculating weighted distances in spatio-temporal space.

One problem of this simple approach is the undesired backward propagation in time. As shown in Figure 6.6(a), two objects A and B are separated on frame t_1, then overlap on frame t_2, and finally separate again on frame t_3. If the user specifies A as foreground and the rest of the image as background, then the foreground label will be propagated to frame t_2, and since A and B overlap on this frame, the foreground label is then propagated backwards in time following B's trajectory, and finally B is segmented as foreground on frame t_1, which is incorrect. A simple solution to solve this problem is to constrain the propagation to be forward-only, as shown in Figures 6.6(b) and 6.6(c).

The nice property of this approach is that since the geodesic distances can be computed in $O(n)$ complexity, the segmentation can be achieved very efficiently, allowing the user to interactively refine the segmentation until it converges.

6.6 Summary

Video matting is inherently a more challenging task than image matting, and the difficulties lie in three aspects: (1) how to allow the user to efficiently specify the dynamic spatio-temporal foreground object in a video sequence; (2) how to propagate the small amount of user input to the vast amount of pixels living in the sequence to generate segmentation that is temporally coherent; and (3) how to develop efficient algorithms that can give users rapid feedback.

Most existing video matting systems adopt a two-step framework by first interactively generating high quality binary segmentation and using it to generate trimaps for video frames, then applying image matting algorithms to generate the final mattes. In the segmentation (trimap generation) step a number of techniques have been explored to efficiently segment the entire video based on small amount of user input, such as optical flow, rotoscoping, graph-cut optimization, and the computation of geodesic distances. In the matting step the matte is often encoded with strong prior profiles to ensure matte estimation to be less erroneous when dealing with similar foreground and background colors.

However, as pointed out in [48], this "segmentation + matting" framework will fail when the foreground object presents large amounts of transparent pixels. Most approaches will dilate the binary segmentation boundary by 10–20 pixels to create a narrow band around the foreground for matting, which may not be sufficient for covering all the fine details of the foreground. Additionally, some approaches, such as the rotoscoping system [2] and the cutout system [47], require matching foreground boundaries across frames, thus will not be able to handle objects with fast-changing topologies or occlusions very well.

7

Matting with Extra Information

7.1 Motivation

As addressed in Section 1.1, matting from a single image or video sequence is a severely under-constrained problem, since 7 unknown variables need to be estimated from 3 known ones for every unknown pixel. Knowing or having a close guess of any of the unknown variables ahead of time will significantly reduce the size of the solution space, typically resulting in more accurately estimated mattes. Many approaches have been proposed to utilize such extra information for matting when it is available, both in the image domain and the video domain.

Unfortunately, the extra information does not come free. It may require specially designed capturing devices, or require capturing an object using different camera settings over multiple shots. In this section we review some of the system designs for such a purpose.

7.2 Blue Screen Matting

In early matting approaches, the problem is simplified by having the foreground object to be shot against one or multiple known constant-colored background(s), which is called *blue screen matting*. Note that in this setup, although the background is a constant-colored scene, the exact background color for an unknown pixel is still unknown (although good estimations can be made fairly easily) due to the effects of shadows and non-perfect lighting conditions.

Smith and Blinn [37] showed that simple constraints make the problem tractable, by assuming that $0.5 \leq \alpha_2 \leq F_b \leq \alpha_2 F_g$, where F_b and F_g are blue and green channels of the foreground color, and α_2 is a user-selected parameter. Under this assumption the alpha value can be computed as

$$\alpha = 1 - \alpha_1(I_b - \alpha_2 I_g), \tag{7.1}$$

where α_1 is another user-controlled parameter, and I_b and I_g are blue and green channels of the observed pixel. This approach, while easy to implement, requires an expert to tune the parameters and can fail on fairly simple foregrounds.

A more useful technique derived from this work is *triangular matting*, which has been used in many recent matting approaches as part of the methodology for generating ground-truth mattes [22, 49]. In the simplest situation, if the foreground is shot against two different shades of blue color, for a foreground color $F_z = [F_r, F_g, F_b]$, its two observed colors are $[I_{r_1}, I_{g_1}, I_{b_1}] = [F_r, F_g, F_b + (1 - \alpha_z)B_{k_1}]$ and $[I_{r_2}, I_{g_2}, I_{b_2}] = [F_r, F_g, F_b + (1 - \alpha_z)B_{k_2}]$, then α_z can be solved as $1 - (I_{b_1} - I_{b_2})/(B_{k_1} - B_{k_2})$ (since $B_{k_1} - B_{k_2} \neq 0$). This can be generalized to foreground objects shot against any two distinct background colors C_{k_1} and C_{k_2}, where both are arbitrary and $(R_{k_1} - R_{k_2}) + (G_{k_1} - G_{k_2}) + (B_{k_1} - B_{k_2}) \neq 0$, the solution for α_z is

$$\alpha_z = 1 - \frac{(I_{r_1} - I_{r_2}) + (I_{g_1} - I_{g_2}) + (I_{b_1} - I_{b_2})}{(R_{k_1} - R_{k_2}) + (G_{k_1} - G_{k_2}) + (B_{k_1} - B_{k_2})}. \tag{7.2}$$

These conditions are quite broad: only the sums of the primary color coordinates of the two background colors have to differ. In fact, a constant background color is not necessarily required.

Another representative blue screen matting is the nonparametric-sampling-based technique proposed in [27], which has been described in detail in Section 2.3.1.

7.3 Flash Matting

Processing flash and non-flash image pairs has gained considerable attention in recent years for a variety of applications such as photo enhancement [15], red-eye correction [28], nonphotorealistic rendering [30], etc. In [39], a matting algorithm based on flash/no-flash image pairs is proposed, based on the observation that the most noticeable difference between the flash and no-flash image is in the foreground object, if the background scene is sufficiently distant. An example is shown in Figure 7.1, where Figure 7.1(a) shows the flash image $I^f = \alpha F^f + (1 - \alpha)B^f$, Figure 7.1(b) shows the corresponding non-flash image $I = \alpha F + (1 - \alpha)B$, and Figure 7.1(c) shows the flash-only image $I^f - I$. Note that the background of the flash-only image is dark, indicating that $B^f \approx B$.

The foreground matte is estimated by using non-flash image I and flash-only image $I' = I^f - I$, in a joint Bayesian matting algorithm. For an unknown pixel, the likelihood function to be maximized is

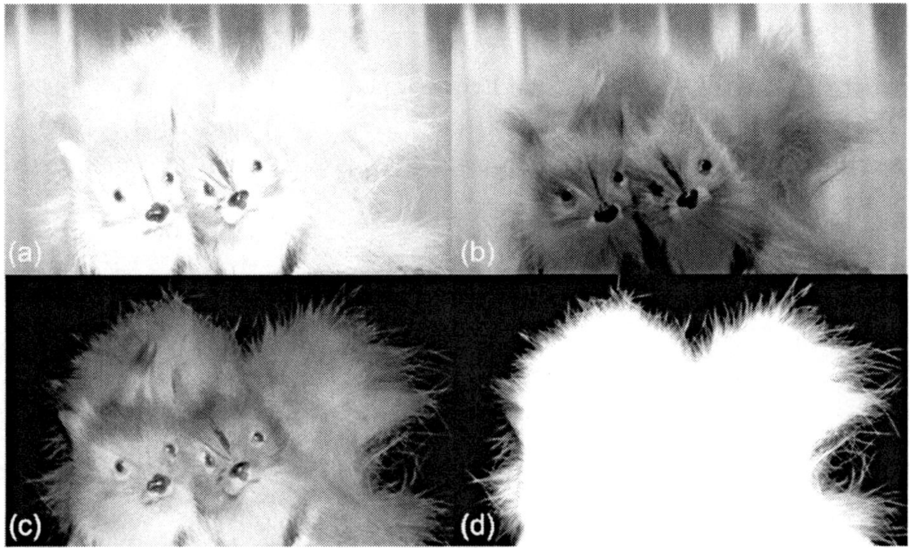

Fig. 7.1 Foreground flash matting [39]. (a) The flash image. (b) The non-flash image. (c) Flash-only image. (d) Extracted matte. Images are taken from [39].

defined as

$$\begin{aligned}
&\arg \max_{\alpha,F,B,F'} L(\alpha, F, B, F'|I, I') \\
&\quad = \max_{\alpha,F,B,F'} \{L(I|\alpha, F, B) + L(I'|\alpha, F') + L(F) + L(B) \\
&\quad\quad + L(F') + L(\alpha)\},
\end{aligned} \tag{7.3}$$

where the first two terms on the right-hand side are defined as

$$L(I|\alpha, F, B) = -\|I - \alpha F - (1-\alpha)B\|/\sigma_I^2, \tag{7.4}$$

and

$$L(I'|\alpha, F') = -\|I' - \alpha F'\|/\sigma_{I'}^2, \tag{7.5}$$

where σ_I and $\sigma_{I'}$ are noise variances which are fixed parameters. The likelihood $L(F)$ and $L(F')$ are determined in a similar way as Baeysian matting [9]: A group of nearby foreground colors are collected as samples and form an oriented Gaussian distribution, thus the log likelihood is calculated as

$$L(F) = -(F - \bar{F})^T \Sigma_F^{-1} (F - \bar{F}), \tag{7.6}$$

where $\bar{F}$ and Σ_F^{-1} are mean and covariance matrix of the distribution. The same method is applied to calculate $L(F')$ and $L(B)$. $L(\alpha)$ is assumed to be a constant. The total log likelihood will be maximized when

$$\alpha = \frac{\sigma_{I'}^2 (F-B)^T (I-B) + \sigma_I^2 F'^T I'}{\sigma_{I'}^2 (F-B)^T (F-B) + \sigma_I^2 F'^T F'}, \tag{7.7}$$

and

$$\begin{aligned}
&\begin{bmatrix} \Sigma_F^{-1} + I\alpha^2/\sigma_I^2 & I\alpha(1-\alpha)/\sigma_I^2 & 0 \\ I\alpha(1-\alpha)/\sigma_I^2 & \Sigma_B^{-1} + I(1-\alpha)^2/\sigma_I^2 & 0 \\ 0 & 0 & \Sigma_{F'}^{-1} + I\alpha^2/\sigma_{I'}^2 \end{bmatrix} \begin{bmatrix} F \\ B \\ F' \end{bmatrix} \\
&\quad = \begin{bmatrix} \Sigma_F^{-1}\bar{F} + I\alpha/\sigma_I^2 \\ \Sigma_B^{-1}\bar{B} + I(1-\alpha)/\sigma_I^2 \\ \Sigma_{F'}^{-1}\bar{F}' + I'\alpha/\sigma_{I'}^2 \end{bmatrix},
\end{aligned} \tag{7.8}$$

where I is the 3×3 identity matrix. α and $\{F, B, F'\}$ are iteratively estimated until convergence.

By using flash and non-flash image pairs this approach can generate good alpha mattes even when foregrounds and backgrounds contain complex patterns, as shown in Figure 7.1(d). However, the limitations of this approach are also obvious. The underlying assumption is that only the appearance of foreground is dramatically changed by the flash, which may not hold in practice. Other possible failure situations include low reflectance foreground, surfaces near silhouettes, and pixel saturation. This approach also assumes that the input image pair is pixel-aligned, thus will fail when the fine foreground structures have moved in the time interval between the two images.

7.4 Compositional Matting

Given an input image, most matting approaches will first try to estimate a foreground matte, which can then be used to recompose the foreground onto a new background to create a novel composite. In this process matting and compositing as treated as separate tasks. The compositional matting system proposed in [50] is the first approach to integrate matting and compositing into a single optimization process, by treating both the original image and the new background image as the input, and taking advantage of knowing the new background image onto which the foreground is to be composed. The key idea of the algorithm is that if the new background has similar regions to the original background, instead of extracting the true foreground matte in these regions which can be difficult, a good transition between the old and the new background can be found for creating a good composite. In spirit, this is similar to the photomontage system [1]. In other words, matte estimation can be conservative in this case and thus some of the original background is carried into the composed image with the foreground.

This approach is also similar to the "drag-and-drop pasting" system [19] where characteristics of both the source and the target images are explored for creating a successful composite using Poisson blending techniques. Specifically, a shortest closed-path algorithm is proposed to search for the optimal location of the foreground boundary, thus

Fig. 7.2 Using the compositional algorithm [50] for foreground retargeting. Left: The original image. Middle: User input. Right: Result image where the foreground is enlarged 1.9 times. Images are taken from [50].

the final composite will contain the least amount of artifacts caused by imperfect boundary conditions. Moreover, to faithfully preserve the object's fractional boundary, a blended guidance field is constructed to incorporate the foreground alpha matte. However, as with other gradient-based blending techniques, the composites generated by this approach often contain strong discoloration artifacts [33], which is often undesirable.

An interesting application of the compositional matting approach is foreground retargeting. As shown in Figure 7.2, using the algorithm the foreground object can be enlarged while maintaining the wide angle view of the background.

However, the system is limited to work well only when the new background has large, similar regions to the original background. Also, since the output of the system is a composite rather than a matte, the system needs to be invoked each time a new background image is selected.

7.5 Defocus Matting

A multi-sensor camera is developed in [26], which captures multiple synchronized video streams, as shown in Figure 7.3. Beam splitters allow all sensors to share a virtual optical center yet have varying parameters. The pinhole sensor has a small aperture that creates a large depth of field. The foreground and background sensors have large apertures, creating narrower depths of field. The foreground sensor produces sharp images for objects within about 0.5 m of depth of the foreground object

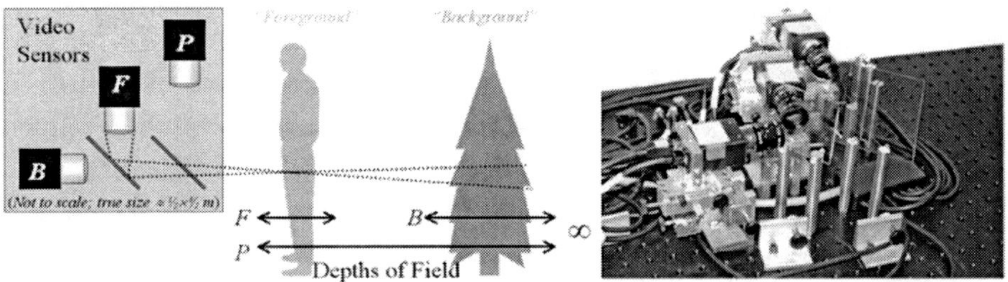

Fig. 7.3 Left: The illustration of the multiparameter video camera used for defocus matting [26]. Right: The actual camera. Images are taken from [26].

and defocuses objects farther away. The background sensor produces sharp images for objects from about 5 m to infinity and defocuses the foreground object.

Given all three streams, matting becomes an over-constrained problem since for each frame, we have 7 unknowns α, $F_{\{r,g,b\}}$, and $B_{\{r,g,b\}}$, but 9 known variables $I_{P\{r,g,b\}}$, $I_{F\{r,g,b\}}$, and $I_{B\{r,g,b\}}$. The actual matte is solved by a rather complex optimization process. A trimap is first automatically generated by classifying pixels to background, foreground or unknown based on their z values. The matte, true foreground and background colors are then estimated by solving a large optimization problem using a gradient descent solver.

The main contribution of this survey is to introduce the multiparameter camera to the video matting problem. The limitation of this system lies in the following aspects. First, as addressed by the authors, the sensors behind two beam splitters receive only 25% of the incident light, thus the system requires stronger illumination than does a normal camera. The system also requires a significant depth discontinuity between foreground and background, and is limited to scenes where the foreground and background are visually distinguishable. This also brings a question mark to the expensive computation involved in the matting process, since in the case that foreground and background are well separable, other simpler matting algorithms may work equally well. It is unclear how the matting algorithm proposed in this approach would compare to other matting algorithms given the same set of trimaps.

7.6 Matting with Camera Arrays

Using a camera array to extract high quality foreground mattes from video sequences has been proposed in [20]. The actual system is shown in Figure 7.4. The key idea behind the system is that relative parallax in the array images, due to separation between the foreground and background, allows foreground objects to be captured in front of different parts of the background. Given a sufficiently textured background, the foreground object can be captured in front of several background colors, which constrains the matting problem.

Mathematically, in the system **I**, **F**, and **B** are all treated as random variables and each camera i ($i \in [1,n]$) captures a sample of them as $I_i = \alpha F_i + (1-\alpha)B_i$. Note that the matte α is assumed to be consistent across different cameras. Taking the variances of the matting equation gives us:

$$\begin{aligned} \mathrm{var}(\mathbf{I}) &= \mathrm{var}[\alpha\mathbf{F} + (1-\alpha)\mathbf{B}] \\ &= \alpha^2\mathrm{var}(\mathbf{F}) + (1-\alpha)^2\mathrm{var}(\mathbf{B}), \end{aligned} \tag{7.9}$$

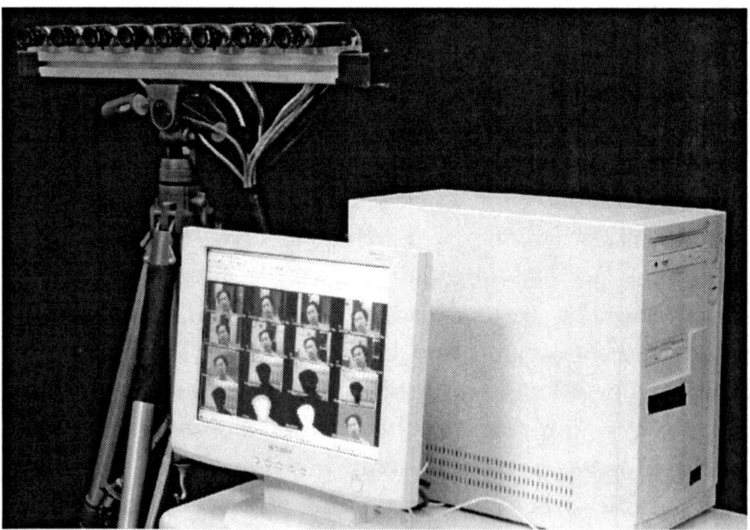

Fig. 7.4 The camera array matting system [20].

by assuming that **F** and **B** are statistically independent. The solutions to the quadratic equation are

$$\alpha = \frac{\mathrm{var}(\mathbf{B}) \pm \sqrt{\Delta}}{\mathrm{var}(\mathbf{F} + \mathrm{var}(\mathbf{B}))}, \tag{7.10}$$

where

$$\Delta = \mathrm{var}(\mathbf{I})[\mathrm{var}(\mathbf{F}) + \mathrm{var}(\mathbf{B})] - \mathrm{var}(\mathbf{F})\mathrm{var}(\mathbf{B}). \tag{7.11}$$

In practice, one of the solutions is often greater than 1, thus needs to be discarded. In case that both are valid, the average is taken as the solution. The final solution is summarized as:

$$\alpha = \begin{cases} 0 & : \mathrm{var}(\mathbf{I}) > \max(\mathrm{var}(\mathbf{B}), \mathrm{var}(\mathbf{F})); \\ \frac{\mathrm{var}(\mathbf{B})+\sqrt{\Delta}}{\mathrm{var}(\mathbf{B})+\mathrm{var}(\mathbf{F})} & : \mathrm{var}(\mathbf{B}) < (\mathbf{I}) \le \mathrm{var}(\mathbf{F}); \\ \frac{\mathrm{var}(\mathbf{B})-\sqrt{\Delta}}{\mathrm{var}(\mathbf{B})+\mathrm{var}(\mathbf{F})} & : \mathrm{var}(\mathbf{F}) < (\mathbf{I}) \le \mathrm{var}(\mathbf{B}); \\ \frac{\mathrm{var}(\mathbf{B})}{\mathrm{var}(\mathbf{B})+\mathrm{var}(\mathbf{F})} & : \frac{\mathrm{var}(\mathbf{B})\mathrm{var}(\mathbf{F})}{\mathrm{var}(\mathbf{B})+\mathrm{var}(\mathbf{F})} \le \mathrm{var}(\mathbf{I}) \le \min(\mathrm{var}(\mathbf{F}), \mathrm{var}(\mathbf{B})); \\ 1 & : \mathrm{var}(\mathbf{I}) < \frac{\mathrm{var}(\mathbf{B})\mathrm{var}(\mathbf{F})}{\mathrm{var}(\mathbf{B})+\mathrm{var}(\mathbf{F})}. \end{cases} \tag{7.12}$$

Discontinuities will occur when switching from one solution to another, but will be small enough if $\mathrm{var}(\mathbf{B}) \gg \mathrm{var}(\mathbf{F})$.

Note that for an unknown pixel $\mathrm{var}(\mathbf{B})$ and $\mathrm{var}(\mathbf{F})$ are still unknown. They are estimated by assuming that the second-order statistics vary smoothly on the image, thus for an unknown pixel z, its variances can be approximated by using the variances of nearest foreground and background samples, i.e., $\mathrm{var}(\mathbf{F}_z) \approx \mathrm{var}(\mathbf{F}_z^f)$ and $\mathrm{var}(\mathbf{B}_z) \approx \mathrm{var}(\mathbf{B}_z^b)$, where F_z^f and B_z^b are nearest foreground and background samples on the trimap.

The system has been demonstrated to be very efficient, and can handle not only hair and trees, but also transparent objects such as fluids and smoke, which is nearly impossible to achieve using the defocus matting system or flash matting system. The light computation enables the system to extract mattes in nearly realtime.

However, this approach also suffers from several limitations. The alpha matte is assumed to be fixed and not view-dependent. However, this is not true for some objects/materials which present self-occlusion.

Also, the variance of the background is assumed to be several orders of magnitude larger than that of the foreground, which may not be the case. The accuracy of the system is also limited by aliasing in the light fields. Finally, the system is specifically designed for indoor scenes with controllable backgrounds, thus it is hard to extend to general outdoor scenes.

7.7 Summary

Given only one input image or video sequence, matting is a severely ill-posed problem due to the large number of unknown variables. Most matting approaches rely on the user to provide sufficient constraints toward good solutions. For difficult examples it is often a tedious process for users to specify accurate trimaps, and the results may still suffer from inaccuracy. The problem is obviously more severe on video sequences than still images.

Matting systems described in this section take a different approach toward accurate and efficient matting, by creating and using extra foreground or background information to constrain the matting problem. Various techniques or devices for capturing extra information have been proposed, such as using flash/non-flash image pairs, multiparameter cameras, and camera arrays. It is shown that once the additional information can be faithfully captured, it can be used to dramatically reduce the user's effort for pulling out high quality mattes from images or video sequences.

These approaches have opened many new possibilities in matting research. However, their practical usage is somewhat limited due to their special requirements on data acquisition. For instance, the flash and non-flash images need to be perfectly registered to recover the fine foreground details. A significant depth discontinuity is required in the defocus matting system, and foreground is assumed to not have self-occlusion in the camera array matting system. These assumptions may not hold in real cases. Looking forward, given the fast evolving of advanced imaging techniques in recent years, one can expect more power imaging systems to be developed in the near future which are as general as regular cameras we have today, but can capture much richer information to significantly reduce the difficulty for high quality matting.

8

Conclusion

The ultimate goal of matting research is to develop intelligent, user-friendly, computationally efficient tools, which can be used to extract high quality mattes wherever the foreground and background are separable to human eyes, both on still images and video sequences. In this survey, we have tried to provide a comprehensive review of existing image and video matting techniques. Many state-of-the-art algorithms and systems have been visited, discussed, and compared. To compare approaches, we explain each method's motivation, why it works, and when and where it will fail.

We have discussed how samples can be drawn from known foreground and background areas and then how these samples have been used to develop models for the different regions. This led to examining how optimization methods use these models to determine the foreground matte. We then have shown a quantitative comparison of many of the published methods. Video matting presents special challenges and opportunities which was discussed next. Finally, we show how some systems have leveraged additional input for the matting problem.

There is of course much more to be done, and new applications to be developed given the recent success of the matting approaches we have outlined.

8.1 Limitations of Current Approaches

Although matting techniques have been largely improved in recent years, there is still a long way to go to finally solve the problem.

8.1.1 Accuracy

Current matting approaches can achieve good results when the foreground and background are smooth and well-separable in the color space. However, if the foreground and/or background contain(s) highly textured regions with complex color patterns, existing matting approaches tend to generate noisy results with noticeable artifacts. In the experiments conducted in Section 5, for the test example $T5$ (see Figure 5.1), the strong texture patterns on the background have caused all algorithms to generate MSE errors that are significantly larger than those generated from other examples (see Table 5.2). One could imagine that a more complex background will make the situation even worse. Strong color discontinuities within texture patterns may be even stronger than real foreground edges, thus will confuse most of matting algorithms. How to improve the accuracy of matting algorithms against such difficult examples is a open question.

8.1.2 Efficiency

As revealed in Section 5, although recently proposed matting algorithms tend to generate more accurate results than early approaches, they are generally more expensive to compute. The Soft Scissors system [46] achieves near-realtime performance on 1000×1000 images, but are not able to give instant feedback on larger ones. The memory consumption of matting algorithms also need to reduced in order to deal with gigapixel images. The GPU implementation for the basic Random Walk matting [16] is inspiring, but how to take advantage of GPU computation for other algorithms is still unknown.

8.2 Future Directions

There are a number of directions that one can explore in order to improve current matting algorithms, or build new matting systems that outperform existing ones. In this section we mention some of the interesting possibilities that we think may inspire future research.

8.2.1 Automatic Evaluation toward Self-Adjusting Mattes

There are some common properties of good mattes extracted from natural images. For instance, the transition from foreground to background are generally smooth, and it is almost impossible to have two neighboring pixels whose alpha values are 1 and 0, or have a region where every pixel has the same alpha value of 0.5. These errors can often be spotted in erroneous mattes.

Developing automatic means that can detect erroneous matting results, both globally and locally, can be beneficial to existing matting systems. Most of existing matting algorithms have a number of tunable parameters, which are either fixed internally, or provided to the user to tweak. If the resulting matte can be automatically evaluated, matting algorithms thus can adjust their parameters to find the best parameter combination, which can generate the best possible result.

Automatic evaluation can also help build hybrid matting system by combining a number of techniques together. As described in previous sections, different matting algorithms have quite different characteristics, thus may work well in different situations. By evaluating results generated by different algorithms from the same input, a better one can be produced by combining all of them together using the best parts of each of them.

8.2.2 Learning/Example-based Approaches

Existing matting approaches only rely on the current input to generate a result, thus could fail in similar situations over and over again. This gives us the opportunity to use example-based learning approaches to augment matting systems, and give them the ability to learn what the correct mattes should be in certain situations. Potentially, a matting system could be customized if the user keeps feeding it certain types of inputs. As more training examples are available one can hope the systems can improve. As a result, the required user efforts for generating good results will be reduced over time.

The idea may sound straightforward, but how to implement such a system remains an open problem. Since foregrounds in different images usually have quite different colors and shapes, the training samples may contain extremely large variances. A compact set of features thus need to be extracted which can capture the essential characteristics of the underlying mattes, while ignoring the absolute foreground and background colors in each example.

The newly proposed high resolution matting system [31] has made the first attempt along this direction. A high resolution ground-truth data set is constructed, and a new gradient preserving prior on alpha is developed based on the training data, which is used in the "alpha deblurring" process for improving the results generated by previous approaches. Such a data set is extremely valuable for exploring new example-based matting approaches in the future.

8.2.3 More Practical Video Matting Systems

A number of image matting systems have already been successfully commercialized. Compared with image matting tools, current video matting systems are somewhat less practical. As addressed in Section 6, existing systems either are computationally expensive, or have too many assumptions which may or may not hold in practice. Furthermore, it is unclear what is the right user interface for video matting. Keyframe-based interfaces are natural and intuitive, but may not be efficient when large motions present. Volume-based interfaces are very efficient for marking foreground objects in multiple frames, as shown in the Video Cutout system [47], however are less intuitive for normal users. A hybrid interface which combines them together may stand out in the future.

8.3 Conclusion

Once a matte has been extracted, what can one do with it? We have barely touched on this topic. The obvious application is compositing the matte and associated image onto a new background, but other applications are possible. We have shown one application for reformatting images by making the foreground object bigger on the same background. One can also envision much more interesting compositing applications where multiple matted images and video are combined. This raises other issues such as adjusting the lighting, color temperature, and shadowing to create a seamless composite. We are sure there are other applications we have not thought of. Hopefully this survey will provide a good basis for those wanting to push the state-of-the-art in matting methods and for developing new unforseen applications.

Acknowledgments

We would like to thank authors of a number of existing matting systems to share their code or executables for generating results in this survey, including Xue Bai, Guillermo Sapiro, Anat Levin, Yu Guan, Wei Chen, and Yung-Yu Chuang. We thank the anonymous reviewer for his/her valuable comments and suggestions.

References

[1] A. Agarwala, M. Dontcheva, M. Agrawala, S. Drucker, A. Colburn, B. Curless, D. Salesin, and M. Cohen, "Interactive digital photomontage," in *Proceedings of ACM SIGGRAPH*, pp. 294–302, 2004.

[2] A. Agarwala, A. Hertzmann, D. H. Salesin, and S. M. Seitz, "Keyframe-based tracking for rotoscoping and animation," in *Proceedings of ACM SIGGRAPH*, pp. 584–591, 2004.

[3] X. Bai and G. Sapiro, "A geodesic framework for fast interactive image and video segmentation and matting," in *Proceedings of IEEE ICCV*, 2007.

[4] S. Belongie, J. Malik, and J. Puzicha, "Shape matching and object recognition using shape contexts," *IEEE Transactions on Pattern Analysis and Machine Intelligence*, vol. 24, no. 4, pp. 509–522, 2002.

[5] M. J. Black and P. Anandan, "The robust estimation of multiple motions: Parametric and piecewise-smooth flow fields," *Computer Vision and Image Understanding*, vol. 63, no. 1, pp. 75–104, 1996.

[6] Y. Boykov and G. Funka-Lea, "Graph cuts and efficient n-d image segmentation," *International Journal of Computer Vision*, vol. 70, no. 2, pp. 109–131, 2006.

[7] W. L. Briggs, V. E. Henson, and S. F. Mccormick, *A Multigrid Tutorial.* Philadelphia: Society for Industrial and Applied Mathematics, 2000.

[8] Y.-Y. Chuang, A. Agarwala, B. Curless, D. Salesin, and R. Szeliski, "Video matting," in *Proceedings of ACM SIGGRAPH*, pp. 243–248, 2002.

[9] Y.-Y. Chuang, B. Curless, D. H. Salesin, and R. Szeliski, "A bayesian approach to digital matting," in *Proceedings of IEEE CVPR*, pp. 264–271, 2001.

[10] D. Comaniciu and P. Meer, "Mean shift: A robust approach toward feature space analysis," *IEEE Transactions on Pattern Analysis and Machine Intelligence*, vol. 24, no. 5, pp. 603–619, 2002.

[11] C. CORPORATION, "Knockout user guide," 2002.

[12] J. Dennis, J. Robert, and B. Schnabel, *Numerical Methods for Unconstrained Optimization and Nonlinear Equations.* Prentice-Hall, 1983.

[13] I. S. Duff, A. M. Erisman, and J. K. Reid, *Direct Methods for Sparse Matrices.* Oxford: Clarendon Press, 1986.

[14] V. Eijkhout, "Overview of iterative linear system solver packages," Technical Report, USA, Knoxville, TN: University of Tennessee, 1998.

[15] E. Eisemann and F. Durand, "Flash photography enhancement via intrinsic relighting," in *Proceedings of ACM SIGGRAPH*, pp. 673–678, 2004.

[16] L. Grady, T. Schiwietz, S. Aharon, and R. Westermann, "Random walks for interactive alpha-matting," in *Proceedings of VIIP 2005*, pp. 423–429, 2005.

[17] Y. Guan, W. Chen, X. Liang, Z. Ding, and Q. Peng, "Easy matting: A stroke based approach for continuous image matting," in *Proceeding of Eurographics*, pp. 567–576, 2006.

[18] X. He and P. Niyogi, "Locality preserving projections," in *Proceedings of Advances in Neural Information Processing Systems (NIPS)*, 2003.

[19] J. Jia, J. Sun, C.-K. Tang, and H.-Y. Shum, "Drag-and-drop pasting," in *Proceedings of ACM SIGGRAPH*, 2006.

[20] N. Joshi, W. Matusik, and S. Avidan, "Natural video matting using camera arrays," in *Proceedings of ACM SIGGRAPH*, pp. 779–786, 2006.

[21] A. Levin, D. Lischinski, and Y. Weiss, "A closed form solution to natural image matting," in *Proceedings of IEEE CVPR*, pp. 228–242, 2006.

[22] A. Levin, A. Rav-Acha, and D. Lischinski, "Spectral matting," in *Proceedings of IEEE CVPR*, 2007.

[23] A. Levin, A. Rav-Acha, and D. Lischinski, "Spectral matting," Hebrew University Technical Report, 2007.

[24] Y. Li, J. Sun, C.-K. Tang, and H.-Y. Shum, "Lazy snapping," in *Proceedings of ACM SIGGRAPH*, pp. 303–308, 2004.

[25] Y. S. Y. Li and H. Y. Shum, "Video object cut and paste," in *Proceedings of ACM SIGGRAPH*, pp. 595–600, 2005.

[26] M. McGuire, W. Matusik, H. Pfister, J. F. Hughes, and F. Durand, "Defocus video matting," in *Proceedings of ACM SIGGRAPH*, pp. 567–576, 2005.

[27] Y. Mishima, "Soft edge chroma-key generation based upon hexoctahedral color space," U.S. Patent 5,355,174, 1993.

[28] G. Petschnigg, M. Agrawala, H. Hoppe, R. Szeliski, and M. Cohen, "Digital photography with flash and no-flash image pairs," in *Proceedings of ACM SIGGRAPH*, pp. 664–672, 2004.

[29] T. Porter and T. Duff, "Compositing digital images," in *Proceedings of ACM SIGGRAPH*, pp. 253–259, July 1984.

[30] R. Raskar, K. Tan, R. Feris, J. Yu, and M. Turk, "Non-photorealistic camera: Depth edge detection and stylized rendering using multi-flash imaging," in *Proceedings of ACM SIGGRAPH*, pp. 673–678, 2004.

[31] C. Rhemann, C. Rother, A. Rav-Acha, and T. Sharp, "High resolution matting via interactive trimap segmentation," in *Proceedings of IEEE CVPR*, 2008.

[32] C. Rother, V. Kolmogorov, and A. Blake, "Grabcut — Interactive foreground extraction using iterated graph cut," in *Proceedings of ACM SIGGRAPH*, pp. 309–314, 2004.

[33] C. Rother, V. Kolmogorov, and A. Blake, "Image blending," Tech. Rep., European Patent EP1748389, 2007.

[34] M. A. Ruzon and C. Tomasi, "Alpha estimation in natural images," in *Proceedings of IEEE CVPR*, pp. 18–25, 2000.

[35] Y. Saad, *Iterative methods for sparse linear systems.* SIAM, 2003.

[36] H. Y. Shum, J. Sun, S. Yamazaki, Y. Li, and C. Tang, "Pop-up light field: An interactive image-based modeling and rendering system," in *ACM Transactions on Graphics*, vol. 23, pp. 143–162, 2004.

[37] A. R. Smith and J. F. Blinn, "Blue screen matting," in *Proceedings of ACM SIGGRAPH*, pp. 259–268, 1996.

[38] J. Sun, J. Jia, C.-K. Tang, and H.-Y. Shum, "Poisson matting," in *Proceedings of ACM SIGGRAPH*, pp. 315–321, 2004.

[39] J. Sun, Y. Li, S.-B. Kang, and H.-Y. Shum, "Flash matting," in *Proceedings of ACM SIGGRAPH*, pp. 772–778, 2006.

[40] R. Szeliski, "Fast surface interpolation using hierarchical basis functions," *IEEE Transactions on Pattern Analysis and Machine Intelligence*, vol. 12, no. 6, pp. 513–528, 1990.

[41] R. Szeliski, "Locally adapted hierarchical basis preconditioning," in *Proceedings of ACM SIGGRAPH*, pp. 1135–1143, 2006.

[42] R. Szeliski and H. Y. Shum, "Creating full view panoramic mosaics and environment maps," in *Proceedings of ACM SIGGRAPH*, pp. 251–258, 1997.

[43] J. K. Udupa and S. Samarasekera, "Fuzzy connectedness and object definition: Theory, algorithms, and applications in image segmentation," *Graphical Models and Image Processing*, vol. 58, pp. 246–261, 1996.

[44] P. Villegas and X. Marichal, "Perceptually-weighted evaluation criteria for segmentation masks in video sequences," in *IEEE Transactions on Image Processing*, vol. 13, pp. 1092–1103, 2004.

[45] L. Vincent and P. Soille, "Watersheds in digital spaces: An efficient algorithm based on immersion simulations," in *IEEE Transactions on Pattern Analysis and Machine Intelligence*, vol. 13, pp. 583–598, 1991.

[46] J. Wang, M. Agrawala, and M. Cohen, "Soft scissors: An interactive tool for realtime high quality matting," in *Proceedings of ACM SIGGRAPH*, 2007.

[47] J. Wang, P. Bhat, A. Colburn, M. Agrawala, and M. Cohen, "Interactive video cutout," in *Proceedings of ACM SIGGRAPH*, 2005.

[48] J. Wang and M. Cohen, "An iterative optimization approach for unified image segmentation and matting," in *Proceedings of ICCV 2005*, pp. 936–943, 2005.

[49] J. Wang and M. Cohen, "Optimized color sampling for robust matting," in *Proceedings of IEEE CVPR*, 2007.

[50] J. Wang and M. Cohen, "Simultaneous matting and compositing," in *Proceedings of IEEE CVPR*, 2007.

[51] Y. Weiss and W. T. Freeman, "On the optimality of solutions of the max-product belief propagation algorithm in arebitrary graphs," *IEEE Transactions on Information Theory*, vol. 47, no. 2, pp. 303–308, 2001.

[52] G. Wyszecki and W. Stiles, *Color Science: Concepts and Methods, Quantitative Data and Formulae.* New York, NY: John Wiley and Sons, 1982.

[53] C. Yang, R. Duraiswami, N. Gumerov, and L. Davis, "Improved fast gauss transform and efficient kernel density estimation," in *Proceedings of IEEE ICCV*, 2003.

[54] Y. Zheng, C. Kambhamettu, J. Yu, T. Bauer, and K. Steiner, "Fuzzymatte: A computationally efficient scheme for interactive matting," in *Proceedings of IEEE CVPR*, 2008.

CPSIA information can be obtained at www.ICGtesting.com
Printed in the USA
BVOW01s1355271113

337501BV00003B/146/P

9 781601 981349